high-performance culture

ADVANCE PRAISE FOR THE CULTURE QUOTIENT

"In this very compelling book, Greg Besner shows us why culture truly matters. This book will help any leader interested in understanding how culture can truly be a source of competitive advantage"

—FRANCESCA GINO, Harvard Business School Professor; author,
Rebel Talent Why It Pays to Break the Rules at Work and in Life

"Greg does a wonderful job summarizing the why, what and how of a strong company culture. It's brilliant in its simplicity, yet powerful in its application filled with actionable examples. *The Culture Quotient* is the culture leadership handbook that everyone should read."

RUDY KARSAN, Former CEO of IBM Kenexa

"*The Culture Quotient* has great stories, great science and great practical advice about how to build a high-performance culture."

FRED MOSSLER, Employee #1 of Zappos.com

"*The Culture Quotient* is the perfect blueprint for aligning culture with business strategy in a world filled with distraction. It should be required reading for all teams, managers and aspiring leaders who seek real-life examples and solutions to build trust with their team, foster an environment based on truth, and truly use culture to drive business success."

ERIC HIPPEAU, Former CEO of The Huffington Post
and Former Chairman & CEO of Ziff-Davis

"Greg Besner has written a groundbreaking book sharing his valuable learnings as a business leader, professor, and lifelong student of leadership. *The Culture Quotient* shares essential data, pertinent stories, and so many great takeaways and tips. I've already started sharing this book with all of my companies."

BRETT HURT, CEO of Data.World and Former CEO of Bazaarvoice;
Author, *The Entrepreneur's Essentials*

"In his book, *The Culture Quotient,* Greg Besner offers all of us a leadership roadmap we should consider very seriously: to have a resilient company 'Culture' does matter and there are practical ways to align our business purpose and our people values to every aspect of the enterprise! *The Culture Quotient,* and the 10 dimensions described in this book, are a must read for the leaders of small and big companies."

RINO PIAZZOLLA, AXA Global, Retired Chief Human Resources Officer

"In *The Culture Quotient,* Greg Besner has captured foundational principles to create a healthy, positive workplace. Why do some companies have "magic" while others have disgruntled employees? That "X" factor can now be labeled The Culture Quotient. Bringing openness, transparency, and clear expectations helps people focus and find fulfillment. *The Culture Quotient* is a must read for entrepreneurs and business leaders."

JONATHAN D. HARBER, NYU Steinhardt School of Culture, Education, and Human Development Adjunct Professor

THE
CULTURE
QUOTIENT

GREGORY BESNER

THE
CULTURE
QUOTIENT

TEN DIMENSIONS
OF A HIGH-PERFORMANCE CULTURE

IDEAPRESS
PUBLISHING

IDEAPRESS
PUBLISHING

Special Sales

Ideapress Books are available at a special discount for bulk purchases, for sales promotions and premiums, or for use in corporate training programs. Special editions, including personalized covers, a custom foreword, corporate imprints, and bonus content are also available.

DEDICATION:

For you, Mom. I miss you.

CONTENTS

TEN DIMENSIONS:

TONY HSIEH

Author of *New York Times* #1 Bestseller
Delivering Happiness and Zappos.com CEO

GREG BESNER AND I FIRST MET DURING THE EARLY DAYS OF ZAPPOS AND BECAME CLOSE FRIENDS. Soon after, Greg joined the Zappos team as one of our early investors and remained closely involved during the evolution of our company. Today, we still sell shoes — as well as clothing, handbags, accessories, and more. That "more" is always striving to provide the very best customer service and customer experience while making company culture the #1 priority of the company. Greg took inspiration from his involvement at Zappos and found his own purpose: to help organizations around the world create high-performing cultures to achieve their business goals. With his book, *The Culture Quotient,* Greg shares his formula to help you, your team, and your company achieve your purpose, too.

More and more leaders today are recognizing company culture as a top priority because of its long-term impact on company performance. Without it, companies will struggle to deliver happiness to all of their stakeholders. The 2020s and beyond are about delighting customers and engaging employees through a daily commitment to each organization's purpose and core values. When given the choice, customers will select other products and services if they sense that your culture isn't trustworthy or that you are not living your values. *The Culture Quotient* is a systematic approach to culture that will guide you every step of the way as you make your culture a top priority.

Culture is core values in action. Companies that stay true to their values will win the battle for talent, achieve high levels of employee engagement, and ultimately win the hearts and minds of customers. As Greg's book illustrates, culture touches every aspect of a company's management and practice. And Greg's book directly addresses the toughest question in the world of culture: How do you use culture to drive meaningful business results? Answer: Read this book and access the additional resources available online to learn how.

Business leaders have been seeking a practical yet data-driven solution for managing culture for a long time. I hope you enjoy reading *The Culture Quotient* as much as I did.

WRITE YOUR OWN CULTURE STORY

HOW DID I BECOME SO FOCUSED ON CREATING GREAT CULTURE IN THE WORKPLACE? I would love to say I always knew that culture would be an important tenet of my leadership while building several high-growth companies. However, my interest actually started seventeen years ago with a chance meeting in an elevator.

My career set out on a traditional leadership path. During the first decade I worked in Fortune 500 companies, earned my MBA from Wharton School of the University of Pennsylvania, and eventually became a divisional president of a large public company. But for the next twenty years, my career shifted. I found career passion as an entrepreneur building companies, as an adjunct professor teaching at New York University Stern School of Business, and most recently as the founder and CEO of CultureIQ, a company that helps organizations create high-performing cultures to achieve their business strategies.

In 2003 I founded and served as CEO of Restricted Stock Systems, a software company based in Princeton, New Jersey. I was in San Francisco visiting a close friend, Erik Moore, the founder of venture fund Base Ventures, when an elevator door opened, and in walked a guy wearing a Zappos.com T-shirt. Erik introduced me to Tony Hsieh, CEO of Zappos.com and author of the *New York Times* #1 BestSeller, *Delivering Happiness*. I thought nothing of it. At the time Zappos had fewer than seventy employees, and most people, including myself, had never heard of the company or Tony. Today Tony is a business and culture celebrity. (Coincidence: Erik met Tony in 1999 in the same elevator.) If you are not familiar with Zappos, it started in 1999 as a fledgling online site for shoes and today is a multibillion-dollar ecommerce success story.

Just before that chance meeting, I had co-founded a fashion accessories company to design and distribute UGG® Australia handbags. Tony and I kept in touch, and I learned that Zappos was expanding beyond shoes and focusing on handbags. In the next few years, my company became the largest supplier of handbags to Zappos. Tony and I became close friends, and I visited Zappos more frequently. I was so inspired by the company's culture that I decided to join the Zappos team as one of its early investors. Over the next seventeen years, I witnessed firsthand how its culture helped Zappos inspire its employees and grow an amazing brand. Its unique and evolving culture was the critical ingredient to growing from a start-up with sales of $1.6 million in 2000 to many billions in annual sales today.

During a visit to Zappos headquarters in Las Vegas, Nevada, I noticed a bustling bake sale in the main lobby. A crowd of Zapponians (the nickname for employees) were waiting in line to support the sale. Other Zapponians were sitting at portable tables, taking turns selling little bags of homemade cookies, cakes, and other treats. The scene was showing so much positive energy, but I was wondering why a billion-dollar company would be having a bake sale.

As I approached, I noticed photographs of electric massage chairs with a sign noting the target money needed to buy two. I asked the friendly folks behind the tables why they were holding the fundraiser. The answer was heartwarming. It turned out that the workers in the Las Vegas office, mostly call center staff, product buyers, and management, were rallying to buy massage chairs for the Zappos warehouse workers in Louisville, Kentucky.

The Las Vegas team knew that the holiday shopping season was approaching and recognized that their warehouse co-workers would be experiencing tremendous physical labor. Zappos' annual revenue had surpassed $1 billion before the bake sale, so the Zapponians could have requested budget approval to buy the chairs. Instead, they wanted to roll up their sleeves to support their colleagues. Most of the Las Vegas employees never had met their Louisville counterparts, but they decided to pursue this grand gesture to show empathy and appreciation for their co-workers. What a wonderful example of team building from afar!

My involvement with Zappos inspired me to launch CultureIQ seven years ago to help many other companies create high-performance cultures that align with their business strategies. Since then I'm proud that my company has worked with more than one thousand companies around the world. My work would be much easier if there were one secret ingredient to culture, a quick fix for driving engagement and encouraging high performance. Instead, when it comes to culture, as with many things, my best education has come from listening. I believe that great culture can be inspired anywhere, even in an elevator.

I've written this book with three main goals in mind. My first is to spark inspiration. I hope that you feel excited and compelled to take steps to strengthen the culture at your own organization, regardless of your industry, tenure, or role. My second goal is to provide tangible data, tips, and ideas to help you curate your own culture. And third, I want to share inspiring stories from other leaders that show the power and results of culture initiatives in action. The quotes you read in this book are excerpted from original culture stories written exclusively for this project and designed to become a resource for readers and their organizations. While I excerpt the key points and stories in the book, you can read the full transcripts at www.theculturequotient.com.

I'm confident that you will take action to build the ideal culture at your own company if you haven't already. Please share your culture story with me and other leaders wherever your story takes you. After all, you never know where you may inspire great culture, perhaps even in an elevator.

ABOUT CULTURE

WHEN I FOUNDED CULTUREIQ IN 2013, I INTERVIEWED HUNDREDS OF CEOS AND OTHER BUSINESS LEADERS, ASKING THEM TO DESCRIBE THEIR IDEAL COMPANY CULTURE. All of these leaders expressed a strong desire to achieve a high-performing culture at their companies, yet most didn't have a framework to define their culture. As a CEO, business professor, and serial entrepreneur, I have personal experience and research that confirm culture's dramatic impact on an organization, yet most leaders lack a proper definition and effective toolkit to manage their culture.

Flash forward seven years, and it is nearly impossible to read a business publication or attend a leadership conference without finding company culture topics highlighted. Recent Deloitte research compiled from three thousand three hundred leaders across one hundred six countries found that company culture and employee engagement are the most important human capital challenges confronting organizations around the world.[1]

In this chapter, I will provide a practical definition of company culture and employee engagement. I'll explain how these two concepts relate to each other and to your organization. I'll also share data that illustrate the connection between company culture and business outcomes.

WHAT IS COMPANY CULTURE?

Company culture, also known as organizational culture, refers to how and why things get done in your organization. Specifically, your organizational culture reflects your environment, which is made up of the behaviors, values, office rituals, and language of those employed in a workplace.

This simple definition clarifies how culture affects not only employees' relationship to their work, but also how they work. In this understanding, it is clear why it is important to factor company culture into business strategy. Defining culture in this way encourages leaders to view it as a business topic rather than only a human resources issue.

I have learned from a number of academic models that inform this definition of company culture. I like one particularly influential model: the "Three Levels of Culture" that Edward Schein identified in his book *Organizational Culture and Leadership.*[2]

Schein breaks down culture into three layers: artifacts, espoused beliefs and values, and basic underlying assumptions. It can be helpful to visualize these layers as an iceberg, where the artifacts are the tip of the iceberg that we see, the espoused beliefs and values are the part of the iceberg just under water, and the basic underlying assumptions form the deepest part of the iceberg. The corresponding image visualizes this analogy.

What We See	Behaviors, systems, processes, policies
What We Say	Ideals, goals, values, aspirations
What We Believe	Underlying assumptions

All organizations inherently possess a culture. This book addresses these questions: What makes one culture better than another? How do you know if your culture is headed in the right direction? How can your culture drive your desired business results? One way to answer these questions is to understand a high-performance culture.

WHAT IS A HIGH-PERFORMANCE CULTURE?

A high-performance culture is a set of behaviors and norms that enables an organization to achieve superior results, including high financial returns, leading customer ratings, and the ability to recruit and retain top talent. In other words, it is a culture that drives a high-performance organization, one that remains competitive in the financial and employer market. While it is hard to argue the desirability of a high-performance culture, it can feel ambiguous, begging the question: What does a high-performance culture look like?

To answer this question, we can turn to research gathered from our company's work with more than one thousand organizations, as well as gold-standard research conducted by the Boston Consulting Group and Cornell University School of Industrial and Labor Relations.[3,4] After years synthesizing this information, I have identified ten dimensions common to high-performance cultures, in no particular order:

1. **Mission and Value Alignment:** Employees know, understand, and believe in the company's mission and values.

2. **Communication:** Employees send, receive, and understand the necessary information.

3. **Responsibility:** Employees are accountable for their actions and have the independence and empowerment to make decisions regarding their work.

4. **Agility:** The company responds and adapts to opportunities.

5. **Work Environment:** The company has a comfortable workplace where people have the resources to be effective in their work.

6. **Innovation:** The company encourages new ideas, and individuals can move ideas through the organization.

7. **Wellness:** The company prioritizes policies and resources to help people maintain physical and mental health.

8. **Performance Orientation:** Employees know what determines success in their role, and they are rewarded or recognized for achievements.

9. **Collaboration:** Employees cooperate, share, and work well together.

10. **Support:** Employees provide one another with the resources and guidance they need to succeed. Employees are confident in company leadership.

Whether you are building a culture from scratch, trying to determine whether you are on the right track, or looking to make drastic organizational changes, these ten dimensions include every level of the Schein iceberg model and can be measured. They are dynamic, in that improvements in one dimension can improve other dimensions. You can measure these dimensions to track your own culture over time. For example, if you find that your company scored poorly on work environment, you know to focus on this dimension to effect positive change.

These dimensions also prove that you do not need to be Google or Zappos in order to achieve a high-performance culture. A helpful analogy is to think of these ten elements as the key ingredients for creating a high-performance culture and to recognize that every organization has a unique recipe to achieve its designed culture. Another perspective is that your approach to these qualities becomes the personality of your company. When you score your progress, it will help you understand whether your company personality is growing with your organization and contributing to a happy, engaged, and effective workforce.

This book also tackles the toughest question for culture management, where many culture strategies come up short: How does company culture drive your desired business results? Employee engagement is a big part of the answer.

WHAT IS EMPLOYEE ENGAGEMENT?

Employee engagement refers to how employees feel about their company and their work. While this definition might seem abstract, engagement can have powerful results. When workers are engaged, they are more likely to be happy, motivated, and committed to your company. Engaged workers are also more connected to the company's mission, motivated to exceed their goals, proactive about learning new skills, positive in their approach to work, creative in solving problems, and committed to developing their careers at your organization.

With such results, it is no wonder that employment engagement has received so much attention recently. In fact, the term has experienced an eleven-fold increase in popularity as measured by Google Trends over the past ten years. Business leaders, managers, and human resources professionals alike are looking for the best ways to engage their people.

So how do you create employee engagement at your organization? Engagement is an outcome of a high-performance company culture. High-performance cultures outline behaviors and norms that are healthy and supportive, ensuring that team members clearly understand their culture and what is expected of them. Employees feel aligned, connected, and supported, and therefore they feel engaged with their company.

Because culture and engagement are so closely tied, it is nearly impossible to separate the results of engagement from those of culture. In the next section, I will share some of the research about how culture and engagement drive powerful business results.

THE LINK BETWEEN COMPANY CULTURE AND BUSINESS RESULTS

Many people can summon an anecdotal connection among engagement, culture, and success. However, you and your management team expect facts and data to support this link. Fortunately, academics and business analysts have been studying the link between company culture and business outcomes for quite some time. For this book, I have gathered a series of compelling studies that represent the breadth--from employee retention to stock market returns--and the depth of culture's impact on business performance.

The most notable studies come from Gallup's periodic *State of the American Workforce* report.[5] The 2017 report found that that business units with more satisfied employees tend to have higher productivity (17 percent higher), greater profitability (21 percent higher), and superior sales results (20 percent higher).

Gallup also found that the more disengaged employees feel from their jobs, the more likely they are to leave. Nearly three-quarters of disengaged employees are actively looking for jobs, compared with a little more than one-third of engaged employees, according to Gallup.[6] As many leaders know, employee turnover hurts your business. Replacing an employee costs your company an average of $4,129, according to the Society for Human Resource Management (SHRM).[7]

Happy employees typically lead to happy customers, SHRM and others have found. Business units with engaged workers see 10 percent higher customer metrics. Customer satisfaction is directly linked to employee satisfaction, and financial success is directly linked to customer satisfaction, according to Washington State University research.[8] Therefore, employee engagement is linked to financial performance. Similarly, in a study of one hundred organizations, Northwestern University researchers found that companies with satisfied employees also had a higher percentage of satisfied customers.[9] These customers purchased the company's products more frequently, maintained higher levels of loyalty, and reported greater satisfaction, which directly contributed to higher gross margins, higher repeat business, and reduced customer acquisition costs for each company.

Employee engagement also is linked to discretionary effort. One Corporate Leadership Council study of fifty thousand employees from fifty-nine organizations found that 71 percent of companies with an above-average percentage of highly committed employees performed better than average compared with their industry peers, while 62 percent of companies with a below-average employee commitment performed below average.[10]

A study published in the book *Corporate Culture and Performance* by John Kotter and James Heskett details the difference between companies with performance-enhancing cultures and those without performance-enhancing cultures over eleven years.[11] The firms with performance-enhancing cultures achieved four times greater revenue growth, twelve times greater stock price growth, and seven hundred fifty-six times greater net income growth. More recently, the Great Place to Work Institute found that public companies identified as the "best places to work" performed nearly twice as well as the cumulative stock market results of the S&P 500 and Russell 3000 indexes.[12] Your investment in creating a positive place for your employees can literally pay off.

WHERE DO YOU START?

I recommend that you start by understanding your culture. Ask yourself the tough questions: How are things getting done at my organization? How are employees relating to each other, to their managers, to our customers? What are some of the norms, intentional or not, dictating these behaviors? Refer to the models explained earlier in this chapter, measure the strength of the ten culture dimensions in your organization, and most importantly, ask those around you how they feel. Your other leaders, managers, and individual contributors will have the answers you need to embark on your culture journey.

And of course, read on. I created this book to serve as inspiration for all those looking to make a positive impact on their culture. The book provides examples of how leaders approach culture in their organization and the amazing results they can achieve.

CHAPTER 1:

MISSION AND VALUE ALIGNMENT

EVERY SPRING SEMESTER I TEACH A GROUP OF FUTURE LEADERS AT NYU STERN SCHOOL OF BUSINESS ABOUT WHAT IT TAKES TO BUILD A COMPANY. These students are eager to execute their product ideas and build the next Google from their dorm room. Before we jump into lessons on creating a business plan and fundraising, I first focus on building a company culture, starting with creating your mission and values. I do this to emphasize the critical role these pillars play in the success of a business, a thesis backed not only by my own experience but also by data.

CultureIQ data found mission and value alignment to be a top-three driver of employee engagement.[13] Alignment is especially important here. Any company can have a compelling mission and set of core values. The companies with engaged employees are those that put their mission and values into action every day and across all levels of the organization.

Mission and value alignment begin with having a defined purpose that provides meaning to work. Leading organizations also have stated values that represent deeply held beliefs and expected behaviors. Together, the mission and values compose the company's unique identity and reason and way of operating. In a company with strong mission and value alignment, all employees know the mission and values, understand how they connect to their individual work, and see the mission and values consistently followed in day-to-day operations.

Before going further, let's define what I mean by a company's mission and values.

MISSION STATEMENT

A company's mission or vision statement is a clear and concise definition of its single most important purpose as a business. It should answer: What do we do, and why do we do it? It's what every project, initiative, and team goal should link up to. At CultureIQ, our mission is: To partner with organizations and their leaders to make culture a competitive advantage. Here are additional examples of company mission statements:

IKEA[14]: To create a better everyday life for the many people.	SLACK[15]: To make work life simpler, more pleasant, and more productive.
SQUARESPACE[16]: To make beautiful products that help people with creative ideas succeed.	WARBY PARKER[17]: To offer designer eyewear at a revolutionary price, while leading the way for socially conscious businesses.
ZAPPOS: To Live and Deliver WOW.	

Mission statements help employees understand what their work contributes to on a grander scale—beyond the PowerPoints and spreadsheets. My advice is to worry less about the technicalities and to focus on creating and consistently communicating a guiding star that both motivates and unifies employees.

COMPANY VALUES

Core values are the guiding tenets of a company. If a mission defines what we do and why we do it, core values express how we do it.

The most successful values support the company's mission, shape its culture, and reflect its identity. Because each organization is unique, there are no universal core values. Instead, a company must decide what principles it holds most important. Below are some examples:

IKEA KEY VALUES[18]:	
Togetherness.	Caring for people.
Cost consciousness.	Simplicity.
Renew and improve.	Different with a meaning.
Give and take responsibility.	Lead by example.

ZAPPOS CORE VALUES[19]:	
Deliver WOW through service.	Embrace and drive change.
Create fun and a little weirdness.	Be adventurous, creative, and open-minded.
Pursue growth and learning.	Build open and honest relationships with communication.
Build a positive team and family spirit.	Do more with less.
Be passionate and determined.	Be humble.

Every decision an employee makes is an opportunity to apply the company's values. While values can take many shapes and sizes, the best ones make a clear link to how individuals can use them.

HOW DOES A COMPANY AGREE ON ITS VALUES?

A few months after launching CultureIQ, I excitedly shared with my team a first draft of our company's mission statement and core values. I wanted their support and buy-in on this foundation for our future—after all, we were a culture company.

I was surprised when the team—we had six employees at the time—didn't go wild with enthusiasm. They felt that the core values were wonderful but represented my personal values, not our shared company principles. This wasn't the feedback that I expected, but upon reflection, I realized it was an amazing gift. The team members bought into the need to express our core values, and they wanted to be part of the process to create them.

So where did we start? We began by deciding to hike and camp at a state park in upstate New York and brainstorm about our company values over a campfire.

A few hours of hiking and bonding helped us get into the right mindset for discussing company values. By choosing a setting that was far from home and the workplace, we were able to clear our minds and focus on the task at hand. After hiking for a few miles, setting up lunch, and searching for firewood, we started our discussion as the fire lit up. I sat there with a notepad and let the discussion take its course.

Our process looked like this:

- Throw out an idea and discuss it.

- Write it down if there is potential and continue to discuss.

- Repeat.

Here are some questions that guided our thinking:

- What's important to us?

- What brought us all together and continues to hold us together?

- What will help guide us when we are facing a difficult decision?

- What are the things you like about what we do at CultureIQ and how we do it?

- What parts of our company are we proud of?

Here are some questions that guided our refining:

- We're young. Is this something we'll still believe in five years?

- Is this something that we are willing to base hiring decisions upon?

- Is this something we're willing to base firing decisions upon?

- Is this something we can apply to all aspects of our business?

What was the result?

CULTUREIQ CORE VALUES: (CREATED FIVE YEARS AGO):	
Treat ourselves and customers with respect.	Be creative and resourceful.
Choose great people over great résumés.	Understand metrics, but make human decisions.
Be open to change and maintain flexibility.	Celebrate and enjoy the journey.

So did our initial CultureIQ team create core values that endured? Since the time of our camping trip and campfire brainstorming, our team has grown from six employees to one hundred and six employees. We have worked with more than one thousand customers around the world, and we have completed a merger with another company. Five years later, four values created over a campfire remain CultureIQ's core values.

CULTUREIQ CORE VALUES IN 2020	
Treat ourselves and our clients with respect.	Respect data, but make human decisions.
Be open to change and maintain flexibility.	Celebrate and enjoy the journey.

Here's another way to reach consensus. You can create a "culture manifesto" that walks employees through the mission, core values, and examples of how to apply them. CEO David Rodnitzky did this for his San Francisco Bay Area company, 3Q Digital, in a process that took months. "When I think about culture," Rodnitzky relates, "I think about it through this lens: What culture do we need to be a different type of agency: an agency that actually cares about client success, gives team members incredible opportunities, and generally makes a positive impact on the lives of everyone with whom we interact?

"I believe we've already created a culture that does a really good job of living up to those ideals (though we can always improve). Call it the '3Q Way'—there's no doubt that we are much different and better than the average agency, and that's because of our culture.

"Writing this document has taken many months. It turns out that culture is actually pretty difficult to define. Is it what we expect of each other? What we deliver to clients? What we want to be? What we are today? (It's all of those and more!) Ultimately, as I thought about how to define culture, I came up with four attributes."

1. Our mission.

2. Our focus.

3. Our values.

4. Our promise to team members.

What happens if your values no longer fit? What if values become out of date or out of step with company mission? Companies such as Uber or WeWork needed to rediscover and recommit to agreed-upon values that had the buy-in of employees as well as external stakeholders and influencers.

Because your core values serve as a guideline for how workers operate and make decisions, there might come a time when they no longer serve the company in their current state. Sometimes the remedy is as simple as adding a value, removing one, or adjusting the language. However, some scenarios—such as a merger, a different stage of growth, or a culture transformation—can necessitate a more thorough refreshing of the core values.

Danielle McMahon, former Chief Human Resources Officer (CHRO) of York Risk Services, based in Parsippany, New Jersey, explained how her organization crafted a process for forging new values that would underlie (remember the iceberg) broader efforts at culture change:

"After much internal debate and reflection, leadership determined that if we wanted to continue to grow and evolve, we had to challenge ourselves to come together as a unified York team and create the kind of transformational culture that could take us to a new level," McMahon explained.

"York's mission—to reduce risk and get people and organizations back to health, work, and productivity—served as the foundation of this transformation and as a reminder of why we came to work every day and why we were making this bold move forward.

"We knew that to accomplish real cultural change, we needed to do it from the inside out. Senior leadership recognized the need for transformative action and empowered York's HR, IT, and marketing teams, along with others, to tackle this challenge.

"Our overall approach was a systems approach, meaning we needed to align our culture and values to our overall strategy. The first body of work was to define the culture and our values. Once defined, we needed to align all our systems and processes to fit that culture. How we went about defining our culture was by leveraging our relationship with CultureIQ and gathering data and insights from across the organization using surveys, focus groups, and one-on-one interviews. From this, we were able to determine the aspects of our legacy businesses worth retaining and investing in, and which needed to be retired. We created our new values (CARES: Collaboration, Accountability, Results, Excellence, Standards) and established how those values would build our culture."

At Midwestern software company GadellNet, CEO Nick Smarrelli led his growing team through an "exhausting nine-month process of trial and error" to identify their core values. "We didn't want to have core values that were trite; rather, something that served as the foundation for every decision made as a company," Smarrelli says. "We finally put into words what was driving GadellNet employees: Make an Impact, 100% Responsibility, 0% Excuses, Grow or Die."

LIVING YOUR MISSION AND VALUES

Any company can email its core values, post them on its website, and pin them to its wall. That's the easy part. What is harder and less common is applying your mission and values in the day-to-day experience of all your people.

Data from the CultureIQ Top Company Cultures program highlight just how important and challenging this is.[20] When my team at

CultureIQ compared what behavioral norms are present in companies with the highest-rated culture versus the rest of companies, the
largest gaps were in the following statements: "My company stays
true to our mission and values," and "My company hires people who
align with the organization's values."[21]

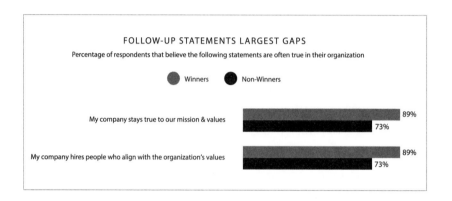

FOLLOW-UP STATEMENTS LARGEST GAPS

Percentage of respondents that believe the following statements are often true in their organization

● Winners ● Non-Winners

My company stays true to our mission & values
89%
73%

My company hires people who align with the organization's values
89%
73%

Hiring for mission and value alignment is arguably the most
important piece of the puzzle to get right. If someone isn't inspired
by your mission or on board with your values, then the employee
won't feel as incentivized to contribute. Further, other employees will
know if a new colleague isn't getting the culture or doesn't care, and
this can tear your company apart.

To prevent this, share your company's mission and values anywhere a candidate might encounter them—in job descriptions, on
the company's "About" page, and during screening interviews—to
demonstrate your commitment and give candidates a chance to assess
their alignment. Then assess every candidate's ability and willingness
to exhibit the values throughout the interview by asking about a time
he/she exhibited each value.

I know this is hard, especially if you are a rapidly growing or
large company. Our research found that the larger the company, the

harder it is to hire people who align with the organization's values. One reason might be that as a company grows, the demand for new talent increases, and recruiters are tasked with quickly filling skill gaps, prompting the hiring to focus more on a candidate's technical skills versus value alignment. If this scenario hits close to home, you might want to consider placing greater emphasis on your mission and values during the hiring process. The same study found that longer-tenured employees give more critical scores to company culture than newer employees. This also suggests the challenges of growing your cultural dimensions as the company expands over time. Longer-tenured employees can become discouraged if the company seems to have lost some of its unique culture.

The *Highlights* children's publishing company, based in Columbus, Ohio, demonstrates how its commitment to hiring for mission and values has kept the company going strong in a challenging industry for more than seventy years. While its leaders don't ignore skills as they hire, they do prioritize a candidate's dedication to the mission.

As CEO Kent Johnson says, "It's far easier to teach craft than it is to teach passion. People who possess the right skills and abilities abound. People who possess both great skills and great heart for the work are rarer and worth holding out for.

"On paper, many employees on our campus may not, at first blush, seem especially qualified for editorial roles at the most widely read children's magazine. Two majored in ancient Greek. Another is certified in environmental studies. Over the years, we've hired a sportswriter, a political science major, English literature majors, an engineer, and a few music majors. But the common, crucial credential on all their résumés was hands-on experience with kids—some of it work experience, much of it volunteer work. And we've found that this makes all the difference."

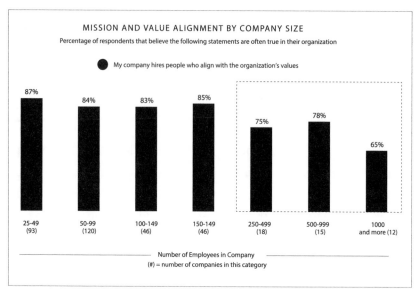

MISSION AND VALUE ALIGNMENT BY COMPANY SIZE

Percentage of respondents that believe the following statements are often true in their organization

● My company hires people who align with the organization's values

87% — 25-49 (93)
84% — 50-99 (120)
83% — 100-149 (46)
85% — 150-149 (46)
75% — 250-499 (18)
78% — 500-999 (15)
65% — 1000 and more (12)

Number of Employees in Company
(#) = number of companies in this category

After an employee is hired, consider the rest of the employee life cycle—onboarding, promotions, ongoing training, termination—and look for ways to embed your values into those touch points. Every policy, process, and program is an opportunity to link back to your mission and values.

RF-SMART, based in Jacksonville, Florida, provides a great example of values-based programming in action. Colleagues nominate someone when they witness that person exemplifying the mission or values. The nominated colleague is rewarded with a $25 gift card and has his/her picture featured on the wall for some time. RF-SMART instills its values into every aspect of the company's operations. According to CEO Michael Morales, the process started with, "What are our values? The time we spent ruminating over our answers led us to a clear, concise mission statement. We all know that some mission statements cause people to roll their eyes, fall asleep, or both. That's why we decided to come up with one sentence that was impactful, accessible, and memorable. That sentence is: We exist to transform our customers and change lives.

"While mission statements are often ineffective, our mission statement truly means something to us. When we talk about changing lives, we can give you examples of people whose lives have been changed because they love their jobs, and even their families feel the impact. We can tell you stories of people whose lives have been changed through our physical, financial, and mental wellness programs. We can even tell you stories of people who have felt so loved and supported at RF-SMART that they would never leave this company.

"I meet with every new hire on their first day of work for one hour to talk about our company's mission, and I share those stories of life change. Many of our leaders start meetings by reminding their team members why we exist. ... I'm confident that if you asked any one of our one hundred seventy-four team members, they could recite our mission statement verbatim and give you an example of how we live it."

Values-based programming doesn't just sound nice; it is actually more effective. A 2016 study by SHRM and Globoforce found that values-based recognition programs had a greater return on investment than recognition programs that are not rooted in values.[22]

In addition to internal programs, your mission and values should guide how you approach external relations. An example is choosing which customers, partners, and projects to pursue. St. Louis-based Contegix shares how the company's vice president of operations applied this thinking when hiring a consultant to run a large warehouse migration. When faced with a failing project and disastrous presentations by two vendors considered leaders in the field, they leaned on their core values to find a new solution.

"My vice president of operations presented all the information to me," relates CEO Matthew Porter. "He emphatically stated that we could not hold up our core values based upon the current execution path. More important, he asked for the chance to take this project on internally and to fire the consultants. This was one of the simplest decisions I have ever made, especially given the weight. It was effectively the question, 'Would I bet on the team that knows our core values, our mission, and our vision whom I hired, or would I bet on strangers?'"

It's no accident that so many CEOs spoke with me about the role of culture in their companies. The most important thread connecting people to the company's mission and values is leadership. Unfortunately, while leaders often recognize the importance of mission and values, they don't always act accordingly. Earlier in this chapter, I shared that eight in ten leaders in a PWC survey believe that purpose is crucial to their company's success. The other, less encouraging part of the story is that only three in ten of these leaders use their organization's purpose as a guidepost for making decisions.[23]

If leaders are not modeling mission and value alignment, how can they expect their workers to take their mission and values seriously?

This reveals to me a huge opportunity for leaders. At every turn—product launches, all-hands meetings, performance reviews, even company picnics—leaders across levels should explicitly link to the organizational mission and values. The data tell the same story. Global accounting giant KPMG found that employees whose managers do not talk to them about purpose are three times more likely to look for another job than those whose managers do engage in such conversations.[24]

Employees should understand what the organization's mission and values mean in a practical sense and how they can apply them to their everyday work, throughout customer interactions, colleague interactions, and product decisions. Not only should this be spelled out for them, but also they should see leaders modeling this daily. This is the difference between simply having a mission and values versus living by your mission and values.

FEATURE STORY:
MISSION AND VALUE ALIGNMENT

American Express Global Business Travel: Culture Week

By Maria Perez-Brau, VP Global Talent Development

American Express Global Business Travel (GBT) formed a new corporate entity in 2014 after splitting from its parent company, American Express. With this change, the company's culture needed to evolve to meet the demands of its new business strategy as part of the stand-up of this new organization. GBT's goal was to build a culture that retained the superior service legacy of American Express while empowering employees to make decisions quickly and encouraging everyone to take ownership of their work.

After defining the company's new strategy and the culture that would help achieve it, GBT identified gaps between the company's current and target culture. To assess the current culture and its evolution over time, GBT partnered with CultureIQ to measure ten dimensions common to high-performance cultures. This provided an in-depth view of the organization as a whole and within various employee segments. The annual survey conducted demographic and benchmark comparisons, comment analyses, and regression driver analyses. The results revealed the culture's strengths, opportunities, and key cultural drivers for engagement.

GBT leveraged the findings to initiate global action planning, refine the company's mission statement, and establish a few key areas of focus to drive culture change. It revealed that after the first year of the new strategies and values being in place, only 63 percent of employees knew GBT's culture values, and only 45 percent believed in those values. As part of the action plan to address this gap, GBT planned and launched "Culture Week," a global initiative focused on building employee excitement and purpose around the company's mission and values.

Culture Week consisted of onsite and virtual activities each day tied to one of GBT's five culture values: Take Action, Win Together, Own the Outcome, Keep It Simple, and Love What We Do. Remote workers participated in photo contests, crossword puzzles, blogs, and videos. Some remote teams planned meetups, volunteer work, and charity runs for team members close enough to join. Each of GBT's office locations planned its own unique activities such as team-building games, recording thoughts on the values on posters around the office, networking breakfasts, decorating cubicles, and sharing their reactions on GBT's intranet, prompting a 60 percent increase in daily page views.

Culture Week proved to be a major success in educating and exciting employees about GBT's new culture. Following Culture Week, the next survey revealed that 88 percent of employees knew the values, and 81 percent believed in them. While significant progress has been made with mission and value alignment, GBT continues to assess progress by regularly collecting employee feedback and using the information to shape and grow the culture.

CHAPTER 1: MISSION AND VALUE ALIGNMENT
TAKEAWAYS AND TIPS

- Ask your team or organization how you are performing respective to this dimension: In a company with mission and value alignment, people know, understand, and believe in the company's mission and values. How would you rate your organization's mission and value alignment?

- Implement a values-based recognition system, where people can nominate their peers for exemplifying a company value.

- Each time you roll out a new program or product, explain the connection to your company mission and values.

- In your employee handbook, provide a set of examples for each value to help employees think through how they are applying your company values to their everyday work.

- Regularly reassess your values by surveying employees. Discuss annually among leaders whether they are still serving you where you are as a company. If not, follow York's lead and adjust your values to match where you need to be as an organization.

- Train your people on making values-based decisions and managers on communicating purpose to their direct reports.

- Create a central location, such as a Slack channel or intranet discussion board, where workers can contribute stories of how their work contributes to the company's mission. This also can be where employees share observations of their colleagues modeling core values.

- Schedule a day, a week, or an event dedicated to your mission and values.

- Create a set of behavior-based interview questions dedicated to determining a candidate's value alignment.

- Encourage candidates to get read up on your mission and values prior to interviewing.

CHAPTER 2:

COMMUNICATION

FOR SOMETHING SO UNIVERSAL, COMMUNICATION CAN BE AWFULLY HARD TO GET RIGHT. In fact, a CultureIQ survey of nearly thirty thousand employees from more than three hundred organizations found communication to be the weakest of the ten culture dimensions discussed in this book.[25] I've experienced this anecdotally as a leader and in my work partnering with clients at CultureIQ. As technology continues to deliver new channels for us to connect, communication in the workplace is becoming both more accessible and more complicated. No longer is it a matter of communicating more; instead, we must focus on communicating more effectively.

What does effective communication look like?

In a company with effective communication, people are able to send, receive, and understand one another and any information they share. This relies on two key components: first, a common vocabulary that allows employees to understand others and any necessary information, and second, the proper channels and processes that enable the information transfer—to and from managers and employees, and within and between teams.

As leaders, it's our responsibility to foster an environment where these communication elements exist, align, and function. We certainly have our work cut out for us, especially as the possible channels of communication continue to expand.

THE IMPACTS OF COMMUNICATION

According to the 2013-14 Towers Watson *Change and Communication ROI* study, companies with highly effective change management and communication are three and a half times as likely to significantly outperform their industry peers than firms that are not effective in these areas.[26]

To better understand these results, it is helpful to consider how communication affects an individual's experience in a company, as well as how it contributes to broader organizational goals and performance.

Communication helps people in a variety of ways. For one, effective communication gives employees access to the information they need to make decisions, creating a sense of safety and certainty while working. Employees are human beings, and we are wired to be socially and community oriented. Our brains trigger fear, shame, and panic if we sense that we are being excluded from a social group. These responses are hardly conducive to motivation, engagement, and teamwork, but they are the result of communication that is false, exclusive, or inadequate. We know this from our own lives, such as when critical family information wasn't shared or when we were "out of the loop" with friends. The enduring cliché testifies to the universal human desire to be told the truth.

At data storage leader StorCentric (formally known as Drobo) based in San Jose, California, leaders needed to overcome a trust problem by implementing a standard way for employees to learn about happenings in the business. The results? Employee engagement skyrocketed, and retention increased.

As CEO Mihir Shah explains, "I was named the CEO of Drobo in 2015, and one of the biggest challenges was creating a culture of trust. The team had always been in the dark about what other departments were working on, as well as the financial condition of the company. There was no transparency. I quickly realized that to get the buy-in from a team, we as a management team had to be open about what was happening, and only then can your team help you be successful.

"We started off with quarterly town halls, but realized that the time in between each event was too long. So we launched a new program called "Transparent Tuesday," which we host every week. We videotape it for remote employees, and almost everyone attends or watches. We also have a small trophy we pass out recognizing one person's contribution for the week."

Communication puts an individual's role and projects into the context of the organization, inspiring workers to feel connected and motivating them to contribute. While increased engagement, retention, and performance each have positive business outcomes, the effects of communication are even deeper on an organizational level. To start, a common vocabulary builds a shared experience for employees across roles, tenure, and teams. Alignment around communication processes reduces inefficiencies and increases productivity. What is more evocative of human potential than language? People are sensitive to how others around them are using language about their roles.

Brett Hurt, the co-founder and former CEO of Austin, Texas-based Bazaarvoice, shares how he established communication alignment internally and what effects it had on his business. He identified how he wanted to communicate and educated his people throughout the company why it mattered.

He hated email, and for good reason.

"I was texting with the CEO of a company I recently backed last night," Brett shared with me. "He used to work for us at Bazaarvoice and knows how important real-time communication is. He says at his company they are using Google Chat as well as their own IRC channel for additional flexibility when needed. But most important, he said they love the accelerated face-to-face conversations in their new office space. And that is the big point here. Instead of wasting time on passive back-and-forth email while trying to get important things done quickly, don't use it unless you expect slow results. Especially don't use it if you know the issue is important, but you are choosing to hide behind email due to your own insecurity or lack of hustle.

"I've seen way too many tasks drag out for days or weeks via email, when they could have been solved with a simple ten-minute, face-to-face conversation. It is way too easy for anyone to fall into this groove and even email back and forth when they sit fifty feet away from each other!"

Further, the success of all other cultural elements and programs hinges on how they are communicated. Consider, for example, that you are rolling out a new performance review process. Managers and employees alike will understand the change, the reasons for it, and the effect for them only if all that information is communicated clearly. Folks will feel comfortable with the change only if they know where to go for questions and answers. And the performance reviews will have the desired effects only if there is mutual understanding of all metrics and terminology.

The CFO of NS Group, based in Newport, Kentucky, explains this interplay best: "For me, with all of the structural changes we made, there was a common thread that allowed those changes to be successful—and that was communication." Quite simply, effective communication is a pillar that makes everything else more effective. So what can you do to tap into all these potential benefits? Learn more from the NS Group feature story.

FEATURE STORY
COMMUNICATION

NS Group: A Tale of Change

By Rene Robichaud, CEO

In 1999, NS Group was dying financially, and the pride of its employees had been sapped by poor operating performance. The board pushed the founder and CEO, Cliff Borland, to bring in an outside executive and potential successor. That June, the company's former investment banker, Rene Robichaud, was hired as president. Eight years later, the company was more profitable than its peers and was acquired for $1.5 billion. Virtually all the 1,500 employees had been able to keep their high-paying jobs.

NS Group was a 140-year-old steel manufacturer that produced cannon balls in the 1860s. By the 1980s, it focused on making steel into steel pipe mainly for oil and gas wells. By 1999, oil traded for around $10 per barrel, meaning NS Group's customers were ailing financially. The company's safety results were much worse than industry averages. Its customers were disappointed in the quality, quantity, and timeliness of delivered product. Employees had filed hundreds of labor grievances against management. Executives stopped walking through the mills. The stock traded as low as $6, a fraction of book value.

The company needed to lower costs. Sacrifices were needed. The question was how to implement needed changes and lift the spirits of a demoralized and angry workforce. We decided to focus on employees by introducing the new, slimmer management team in person. We visited each of the eight facilities in four states every ninety days for the entire eight years. At every session, we spoke frankly about the situation at that facility, gave an update on the company, and said what we planned to do to become successful again.

In essence we communicated more to all our stakeholders than any of them had ever seen. This gave them opportunities to ask tough questions. Employees responded favorably to the new culture we all wanted to see. We defined our culture as the values, beliefs, and habits that would make us successful. Values were standards below which we would never go for any reason. Safety was a prime example. Beliefs were ideas on how we felt the business world works best. For example, we changed our production-oriented beliefs to customer-oriented beliefs.

That was not easy as the founder was a metallurgist who taught all about the virtues of lower costs through high production volumes. We decided to enhance our product changeover capabilities in order to produce shorter runs of products that matched customer demands more precisely. Shorter production runs raised costs somewhat, but our customers responded to our more reliable performance with greater volumes. We implemented many new habits (activities and metrics) that underscored the importance of each value and belief.

We really did not produce a fair financial return for five years. However, attitudes improved considerably by the second year as employees started to see themselves as part of the solution. Our safety improvements came first. The pride that came from a safer environment was the foundation for encouraging employees to enhance productivity and efficiency. These improvements helped morale as we could celebrate each new level of improved performance. Our financial situation was not good, but we stopped the downward spiral long enough for the business cycle to turn. And turn it did. The first quarter of 2004 was our most profitable quarter ever. NS Group's stock was the tenth best-performing stock on the NYSE that year. The year 2005 was better than 2004, and results in 2006 exceeded those of 2005. Employee bonuses in those three years were at record highs. Also important, our margins were superior to our two largest competitors, something that had never happened before.

This financial improvement did not happen because we had the best equipment or technology. On the contrary, the company had some of the oldest equipment in North America for making welded tubular goods. However, when employees put their minds to it, they knew how to make the equipment sing.

Ultimately, the NS Group turnaround came from earning the trust of employees again. This is a process, of course, but was accelerated by a dedicated focus to communicating regularly and honestly with all. The changes in the company's strategy and culture could be fully implemented only with the cooperation of a motivated team.

CHAPTER 2: COMMUNICATION
TAKEAWAYS AND TIPS

- Ask your team or organization how you are performing in this dimension: In a company with great communication, people are able to send, receive, and understand the necessary information. How would you rate your organization's communication?

- Create a process for leaders to share important business updates—a weekly meeting, a company blog, and a roundup newsletter are all options. Whatever you choose, make sure it is equally accessible to all employees.

- Carve out time, space, and processes for staff to ask questions and leaders to listen and provide answers.

- Encourage difficult, transparent conversations, and train everyone on how to have them.

- Be explicit about your norms and create a guidebook that explains them. If you have multiple tools available for use, such as email and Slack, explain the purpose and use cases of each.

- Be willing to adjust these norms as you grow, as new tools arise, and as you monitor how they are used.

- Assume that people do not know and default to overcommunicating. As leaders, it is easy to forget that not everyone operates with the same context and information.

- Enlist managers to help with change and communication efforts. Involve them early and often, and empower them with information.

CHAPTER 3:

RESPONSIBILITY

OUT OF ALL THE CULTURE DIMENSIONS IN THIS BOOK, RESPONSIBILITY OFTEN FEELS THE MOST ELUSIVE TO BUSINESS LEADERS. It is certainly the one that I receive the most questions about. However, when I share what responsibility means in the context of organizational culture, my explanation is almost always followed by enthusiastic nods of "Yes! That's exactly we need at my company . . . so what do I do?!"

If that sounds like you, you're in luck because this chapter provides a road map for this topic. What am I talking about when I explain a culture of responsibility? Responsibility measures the level of ownership and autonomy that people feel they have in their role. Companies that value responsibility provide employees the freedom to make decisions regarding their work and encourage employees to hold themselves and others accountable for their actions.

I like to explain responsibility with the following simple equation:

Responsibility =
Psychological Ownership + Autonomy + Accountability

Viewing responsibility this way makes this incredibly important, yet elusive, dimension more accessible. To build upon that accessibility, in the following sections, I'll break down each variable and explore ways to bring them to life in your organization.

PSYCHOLOGICAL OWNERSHIP

When I started CultureIQ in 2013, I piloted a version of our product among peers in my network. At the time, we referred to this culture dimension as "ownership" in our surveys and analytics. After launching a test version to a peer's manufacturing company, my friend shared that this dimension confused many of his employees. "The staff in the warehouse don't have a financial stake in the company—they don't know how to relate to the question of ownership," he explained.

"That makes sense," I thought. After testing our product with our first group of customers, we decided to change the name of this culture dimension to responsibility because it better expresses the dynamics at play. After all, the goal is for employees of all levels, tenure, and demographics to have the opportunity to feel engaged in their work.

In addition to helping my team fine-tune our initial test product, my friend's feedback got me thinking about how ownership shows up at work for employees. Of course, there is potential for financial ownership among employees via equity compensation, but there is also psychological ownership, which can be just as powerful. I will focus on this type of ownership in this chapter.

Francesca Gino, a behavioral scientist at Harvard Business School, defines psychological ownership as "the experience of possessing and being psychologically tied to an entity." Research demonstrates that feelings of psychological ownership for an organization, regardless of legal ownership, are associated with positive employee attitudes toward the organization, such as loyalty and job satisfaction, and improvements in work behavior, such as performance and organizational citizenship.[27]

Further, Gino's research suggests that when employees feel psychological ownership for a company, they are more likely to engage in prosocial behaviors, meaning they go out of their way to collaborate with and help others.[28] As an old saying goes, no driver ever washed a rental car. We know this is how people operate. When a 13-year-old is given ownership of how the playroom is outfitted, he or she is more likely to keep it cleaned up. We all remember how great it felt as a young employee when we were given our first chance to manage a project or write a memo without a manager looking over our shoulder.

My favorite example of this comes from Hollister Construction. One of the company's values is ownership, and its people take this to heart. According to Christopher Johnson, head coach at the company, "As we continue to grow, we focus on bringing aboard individuals who want to be part of a company that resembles their own personal beliefs on how one should live their life. We also realized that retaining individuals with these values unleashes the best in people and positively impacts the community around us in immeasurable ways."

Hollister organized a culture committee including both office and field employees. "The committee members change after one year, filling the committee with new teammates from different departments and from all levels at Hollister," Johnson writes. "The culture committee organizes monthly events for teammates, families, and communities. From company picnics to friendly sport challenges to philanthropic work and educational seminars, the wide range of events allows the team to cultivate collaboration, build team morale, give back to the community, and share knowledge."

Hollister gives back every year through two company-wide initiatives. More than one hundred sixty Hollister employees volunteer for a single day of action at the Community Food Bank of New Jersey. The second initiative is Hollister's "Dream On" Program, similar to the Make-A-Wish charity, but for internal employees. "Every teammate at Hollister has the opportunity to submit one 'Dream' to the Culture Committee," relates Johnson. "There are no limitations or restrictions on what the dreams can be. The dream can be for a co-worker, family member, neighbor, or anyone else you can think of. The culture committee will then grant dreams and notify the individuals. Initiating this program at Hollister has truly impacted our culture."

Johnson highlighted three amazing employees who exemplify the kinds of initiative that are part of the Hollister culture:

"While working in Newark, New Jersey, we ran into a huge opportunity to help local residents struggling to find jobs. The city offers a tax credit for firms that employ a certain percentage of Newark residents. This can lead to a quick search that yields no results but will render a "good faith" letter from the unions, which allows the credit to be claimed without actually employing the residents. We wanted a real solution and not a letter that said we tried.

"This is where our teammate, Michelle Rogers, assistant project manager, stepped in, took the ball, and ran with it. To solve for not having access to Newark residents' information, we called on a pre-existing relationship at the Mayor's Office of Affirmative Action. Michelle worked with the office to evaluate the information on file, qualify the résumés, and run down the correct information. Hollister does not do the hiring for field workers on projects, but due to this initiative, we have grown into a facilitator between these potential workers in Newark and the subcontractors we hire for our projects. Through Michelle's efforts, we have placed at least twenty people into true employment—not just a job, but a foundation for a future career through this process.

"That is twenty households that are living a different life than before. Our job sites in Newark have become more than that. Now they have the potential to be a job forum for the community.

"Mehul Desai joined the Hollister team, bringing with him extensive knowledge in the construction industry. He had previously taught CAD software classes in multiple countries and even put time aside earlier in his career to teach a foreman how to properly read and extract all the information from drawings. Mehul's passion for sharing knowledge re-emerged during his first weeks at Hollister as he experienced the corporate culture. During a coaching session, Mehul's passion for teaching was discussed, and *The Fundamentals of Construction* class was born. Mehul developed a twenty-week course outline to further educate teammates looking to enrich their construction industry knowledge. The class successfully kicked off in early 2018 with fifteen of our teammates as students. It explored the fundamentals of construction and evolved into a class where guest speakers participated and shared their knowledge. These Tuesday morning classes truly made an impact.

"Five years ago, our teammates Ed Shannon and Chris Johnson were introduced to Al-Tariq Best, founder of the FP YouthOutCry Foundation, a nonprofit in Newark focusing on providing alternative positive programming for youth and families in underserved communities.

"Al-Tariq's most recent initiative is to build The HUBB (Help Us Become Better) HELP Center, a facility offering trauma-informed mental health and healing programs to kids who are survivors of violence. The facility will be the first of its kind in New Jersey providing kids with unique life experience. Learning about this new initiative, Ed Shannon, in a true demonstration of the core values we strive for, took the initiative and planned a daylong event, where we hosted fifty kids from the program for an introduction to the construction industry and a day of fun at Anchor Golf Land, which Ed owns. After exploring our offices, the kids played soccer, drove golf balls, and shot paint balls, all thanks to Ed's gracious donation of his facilities and food."

Just think about it. This isn't a group of Ivy League graduates at a start-up taking a break from their office foosball game to go to the local food bank. This is a construction company uniting its entire workforce of field employees and office staff for major philanthropic work.

With those powerful examples from Hollister resonating for us, let's look at what you can do to realize employee ownership of your culture. To bolster feelings of psychological ownership, you have several options. One obvious path is to adjust financial ownership through equity ownership, but you can explore other ways for employees to direct specific components of their experience and the environment around them.

Committees, for example, provide an opportunity for employees at all levels to drive initiatives from start to finish. One specific example is to seek volunteers to form a committee to plan your annual company party. For employees early in their career who aren't leading any business projects of their own, participating in the committee can give them a sense of ownership over their experience at work. Later in this chapter I provide a longer feature on how to create a culture committee, as one committee example, in your organization.

You can help folks feel in charge of their environment by involving them in workplace decisions, such as naming the conference rooms or choosing the office snacks. Or, as determined by Gino's research, simply allowing people to decorate their workspace to their liking can increase psychological ownership and the associated prosocial behaviors.[29]

Leaders and managers play a crucial role in their team's perception of ownership. Even with a task as simple as filling the copy machine with paper, employees will feel more dedicated if it's theirs to own rather than something they are tasked with completing. Managers have the ability to treat their direct reports' responsibilities as the employees' sphere of control. The opposite of this is micromanaging, which is one of the biggest threats to psychological ownership. Micromanaging tells employees that you don't trust their work, pulling their sense of control out from under them. Our brains actually light up with reward signals and a dopamine release when we have an insight that solves a problem! Micromanaging takes all that away.[30]

This brings up the important concept of trust, which is a crucial underpinning of the next ingredient in the responsibility equation: autonomy.

AUTONOMY

The General Accounting Office conducted a survey of 3,816 mid— and upper-level managers to understand their management challenges. They found that while 63 percent of managers are held accountable for their results, only 36 percent said they have the authority to accomplish their strategic goals.[31]

Sounds problematic, doesn't it? This survey demonstrates a scenario all too common in organizations today. While we want employees to realize their potential at work, we often don't give them enough room to do so. And as Dan Pink writes in his book *Drive: The Surprising Truth About What Motivates Us,* autonomy at work is not something to take lightly.[32] Through his research, he found that autonomy, alongside mastery and purpose, drives employee motivation and often overall business results, too.

In order for employees to experience autonomy at work, they need three things: access to the right resources to get the job done, such as information and tools; a clear understanding of the priorities and decision-making criteria; and (yes, you guessed it) trust from leaders.

Main Line Health, which serves the Philadelphia area, shares how it provides autonomy and psychological ownership to all ten thousand of its employees in a high-stakes hospital environment. They established a clear risk management procedure that empowers all employees to "Stop the Line", which is like pressing a pause button if something seems wrong. In this case, everyone working at the hospital has the authority to speak up for safety.

As CEO Jack Lynch explains, it all goes back to culture. "We began to formally evaluate our safety culture and identify risks for preventable harm in 2009. We determined that while we had many good practices in place, we needed to commit to high reliability practices across Main Line Health to ensure that every patient had the same opportunity to experience a superior outcome. Foundational to our quest for zero preventable harm was the creation of our error prevention tools.

"Two tactics in particular proved most effective in diffusing the power gradient, creating an environment where all staff could raise a safety concern. By using ARCC (**A**sk a Question, Make a **R**equest, Voice a **C**oncern, Use Chain of **C**ommand) and Stop the Line (used to stop any action and reassess the situation so that everyone is on the same page), each and every one of our ten thousand employees is empowered to speak up for safety. Since we launched our formal safety initiative in 2010, this intensive focus has become deeply embedded in our daily practice and is literally saving lives. In 2014 alone, we had a 55 percent reduction in incidents of preventable harm."

Another way to foster autonomy within your organization is to encourage a "coach approach" among leaders. I'm borrowing this term from David Shanklin, an early team member who started CultureIQ's Culture Strategy group. To demonstrate this concept, imagine that an employee goes to his/her manager for help to solve a problem. If managers use a coach approach, they will operate under the assumption that their direct report can solve the problem, and the manager's role is to help the employee uncover the solution. A contrasting method would be to tell them what to do. You can see how guiding and prompting employees to discover their "aha" moment for solving an issue fosters autonomy.

In this chapter's feature story, Jetco Delivery explains how the company uses this approach to manage performance and drive trust.

Even with all this considered, autonomy can be uncomfortable for leaders to embrace. What happens if you trust people to do their work, and employees drop the ball? Autonomy hinges on people doing what they say they will do, bringing us to accountability, the final factor of the responsibility equation.

ACCOUNTABILITY

On one level, accountability in the workplace is doing what you said you would do within the time frame promised. On a higher level, accountability is when people demonstrate responsibility for their actions—assigned or not—and the associated results.

There are two sides of the accountability coin: first, the conditions that need to be in place to set employees up for success, and second, the consequences if and when a responsibility is not completed. Both are levers that you can pull when trying to improve accountability within your organization.

Let's start with the first part. The most important condition is that employees understand the company's goals and how they translate into what is expected of them. Numerous studies confirm the gap between what leaders know and what employees know about what their organization is trying to accomplish. If you notice that your employees aren't doing what is expected of them, a foundational step to remedy this problem is to clarify the employees' responsibilities.

On a related note, employees should understand the impact of their work and how it cascades throughout the organization. Not only will this motivate them to perform their work, but it will also highlight the implications for the organization if they do not deliver their part.

APPrise Mobile, in New York City, turned leaders' and employees' attention to these two factors to improve accountability. At a team off-site, they crafted diagrams to align on inter-team deliverables and dependencies. They found this to be a critically helpful exercise for strengthening team cohesion and engagement.

Now let's explore the other side of the coin. Employees need to understand the consequences of not meeting a responsibility. Sometimes social pressure, (e.g., sending an email explaining that you missed a deadline), provides enough accountability. When the stakes are higher, however, the consequences must be more serious. Houston, Texas-based Jetco Delivery created the "Serious Six" rules, which if violated, could result in serious physical harm or even death to an employee or a member of the public. For violations of the Serious Six, they have a quick and clear escalation process to protect employees and the public.

Finally, employees must feel comfortable having difficult conversations with their peers, direct reports, and managers. Ideally these conversations will catch accountability gaps before they result in more serious consequences. Furthermore, talking these things through might illuminate other factors at play. For example, perhaps the employee wasn't clear on the timeline, or maybe the employee lacked the resources, skills, or confidence to complete the project.

It's worth noting that I am not advocating for a culture of fear. In fact, there is a good deal of research explaining why that approach is ineffective over the long run. Rather, I am advocating for an environment that demonstrates clarity about what is expected and what the consequences are if expectations are not met. In my experience, if the rewards and penalties are fair, this predictability actually helps employees feel safe.

THE COOL CULTURE COMMITTEE PLAYBOOK

It is no secret that culture is defined, driven, and reinforced by the senior leaders. But how do you activate that culture throughout the organization, from the board room to the front line? And who brainstorms events and programs to connect and energize employees and embed the values throughout the organization? Who evaluates what is working, what is not working, and where the gaps are?

The answer: a culture committee.

WHAT IS A CULTURE COMMITTEE?

At the heart of culture lie the organization's core values. Senior leadership plays a significant role in communicating and cascading these values. Human Resources plays a pivotal role in promoting them.

A culture committee is a group of cross-functional culture and organization enthusiasts who continuously discuss, identify, and plan ways to promote, drive, evolve, and maintain culture across an organization, from the top leaders to the front-line employees.

Take Google, for example. The company is a well-known leader in driving and sustaining corporate culture. How did it earn that recognition? By placing a strong emphasis on maintaining culture throughout the organization, stretching from its central office in Mountain View, California, to all other offices and remote employees around the globe.

Stacy Sullivan, Google's chief culture officer, established "culture clubs" at Google. These clubs are driven by employees and consist of volunteers who come together to discuss cultural issues in their office, country, or region. They brainstorm ways to improve culture and continuously keep employees in their areas connected to the broader organization.

CREATING AND CURATING THE CULTURE COMMITTEE

Since culture has a reach to all employees organization-wide, it is important that the committee represents voices from all functions, roles, and levels of seniority. Incorporating this level of member diversity helps to deliver robust insights and ensures that no single function or level has a stronger voice than the others.

When selecting the committee, the goal is to accomplish not only geographical, but also generational and functional diversity among members. Tenure should also be considered. Ensure that members are a mix of longstanding employees, new hires, and all those in between.

In addition, it is important to consider the organization's size and priorities when determining the committee's size. In smaller organizations, this can mean as few as five or six members, as long as all voices are represented. Larger organizations may need a larger committee or more committees to ensure representation based on functions and geography.

While collaboration is fruitful, the committee should not be overloaded with members. Too many participants may make it harder to accomplish goals, hindering effectiveness.

WHO ARE THE IDEAL CANDIDATES?

It is important to seek candidates who have a passion for culture, enjoy connecting with colleagues, love where they work, and promote and embody the organization's core values. Candidates should be allowed to nominate themselves or be nominated by leaders or peers.

Strong communication skills and team player attitudes are must-have traits. Employees who have emerged as natural leaders in their areas of responsibility often fill the role well. Although senior leaders may be tempted to select only people holding key positions or seen as having high potentials, the committee may be more effective if it includes employees who are highly influential and well connected to the organization's informal network.

Candidates should express excitement for their participation on the committee. However, they must have the bandwidth to participate. Employees who are overloaded with other projects and commitments or who have conflicting schedules may see their involvement as simply another task to tackle or box to check.

WHAT IS THE PROCESS FOR SELECTING MEMBERS?

As with any job interview, set standards that the ideal candidate must embody. Encourage committee members to scout for new colleagues who express interest in participation. Ask those who wish to apply to formally indicate their interest and explain what qualities would make them a good fit. In smaller committees, have all members review and vote on the final decision. For larger committees, select a panel of members to review applicants.

Communicate the time and effort required of each committee member during the interview. This ensures that candidates are fully aware of the participation level required.

KEEP IT FRESH!

Because culture is ever evolving within an organization, new ideas and perspectives are of high value. Create committee policies that ensure rotation of members to bring in new ideas and send a cadre of culture champions throughout the organization.

Identify and set the term length for members that best fits the organization. Ideally this would be one to two years. However, this may vary depending on the nature of the workforce. For example, industries with high employee turnover may wish to reduce this time frame. Members should have the option to fulfill several terms when approved by senior leadership.

CREATE A CHARTER

Create a charter that clearly defines the committee's purpose and reason for design. Have company leaders determine what they want the company culture to be? If your desired culture already has been defined, then the committee's purpose should be to help build and maintain that culture. The charter should also include a commitment to evaluating the committee's impact on driving culture within the organization and meeting any goals set forth by senior leadership.

The committee can sponsor fun events, but by no means is it intended to be a social club with the sole purpose of hosting happy hours. Clearly distinguish the committee's mission to help develop and evolve organizational culture in the charter.

Other recommended topics to include in the charter:

- Committee members' responsibilities and roles. Members operate as a voice from their respective departments for colleagues to bring forward cultural concerns and successes.
- The committee's meeting cadence.
- How members are selected.
- Length of member terms.
- Budget resources and uses.

DEVELOP A ROAD MAP

Envisioning and driving organizational culture is similar to developing a product or service. Create a road map for where the organization's culture stands currently and where the committee and senior leadership would like to see it go. Fill in all the steps in between, both those that are easily identified up front and those that are realized along the way.

Understand the culture deliverables that senior leadership would like to identify and achieve, then incorporate the milestones into the road map.

SET A BUDGET

Driving culture within an organization may require financial resources depending on what the business needs and what the cultural road map projects. The committee can best set the budget after considering the events and resources needed, which can vary across organizations of different sizes. You also can also evaluate and evolve the budget yearly to align with the organization's changing needs over time.

MEETING LOGISTICS

To keep all members involved and discussion flowing freely, set up a rotating schedule that grants each member the opportunity to lead a meeting. An additional member should be tasked with taking notes on key points and final decisions. This person will also be responsible for summarizing and communicating actionable steps and information required for the next session.

If employees span multiple offices, ensure that technological resources are available to connect them to the discussion. Web cameras are highly recommended as they heighten remote worker presence and engagement.

Maintain transparency with meeting schedules and to-dos. Although not every note or detail needs to be shared, publish key outcomes from each meeting on your company's intranet site or other internal channel. This will allow employees across the organization to see what the committee is working on and where progress relates to the broader road map. In our era of information overload, keep updates short and digestible in a minute or two.

MEMBER ROLES

The culture committee's ultimate goal is to foster and drive culture within the organization. Each member assumes a responsibility to create excitement and momentum surrounding culture. As a group, committee members seek to identify cultural roadblocks and plan events or programs to promote the desired organizational culture. Members should focus on gathering information from employees across the organization about the current state of culture. This can be done by attending key business meetings or simply by chatting with employees in the hall as they grab a cup of coffee or tea.

Listening to employees gives committee members a front-row seat to the strengths and opportunities surrounding the organization's culture. Whether the topic is brought up casually in the hall or formally at a meeting, questions that members can ask their colleagues to spark the conversation include:

- What do employees feel is working with the organization's culture?
- What does the organization's culture mean to them?
- Are any culture initiatives or events failing?
- What do employees find exciting about working at the organization?
- What energizes employees to come to work?
- Are there any conflicting messages or actions that do not support the culture the organization is striving to achieve?

ACT LOCALLY

For organizations that stretch beyond a single office, create a team of volunteers from each work site or region who are tasked with communicating and promoting culture at the local level.

Local volunteers fill a much-needed role of connecting employees to the broader organization, its purpose, and its culture initiatives. This can involve implementing team events and activities being done at other offices or simply acting as a channel for local employees to voice cultural concerns or pass along ideas to ignite culture in their locations.

Be sure to include remote employees in this initiative. You can task volunteers for remote teams with translating culture-driven events and initiatives into solutions that work well for remote workers. Remember my earlier point: Human beings don't respond well when excluded!

You can host video chat meetings, or if resources allow, arrange an in-person networking event at a mutually accessible location. For any town halls or organization-wide meetings that require in-person attendance, arrange an opportunity for the remote team to connect.

Employees who fill this role should be self-identified culture enthusiasts who enjoy connecting with and listening to their colleagues. Strong communication skills are a must.

Obtain leadership buy-in not only to acquire the necessary resources but also to cascade excitement throughout the organization. With senior leadership backing the committee, employees will recognize the committee's efforts as significant and legitimate.

Ensure the committee has opportunities to present its ideas and initiatives to senior leaders directly, in person when possible. This maintains engagement, builds excitement, and provides a sense of fulfillment for all members.

Promote culture efforts both internally and externally. Intranet sites and internal news blasts are great ways to spread the news regarding upcoming events, accomplishments, and initiatives regarding culture. This extends beyond initiatives created by the committee and includes those from any other part of the organization, promoting or celebrating any new initiatives or programs.

Be sure to share core values and cultural initiatives, directly or indirectly, with customers and other stakeholders. A strong culture is a competitive advantage that should have high visibility.

Develop a brand image for the committee. This goes beyond simply designing a logo or tagline to cultivating a set of dimensions that mirrors the overall organization's values and purpose. Communicate this across the organization via the intranet, bulletin boards in common areas, or email news blasts. Take pride in the brand and promote it.

FEATURE STORY
RESPONSIBILITY

Jetco Delivery: Creating a Just Culture

By Brian L. Fielkow, CEO

As the CEO of Jetco Delivery, a freight and logistics company based in Houston, Texas, I've been fortunate to work alongside my team to create our Driving to Perfection (D2P) culture, which puts safety, accountability, communication, and respect above all else. D2P is a way of life and one that our team embraces.

One of my more inspiring culture stories is when our team moved from a traditional discipline HR system to a "just culture." In my opinion, a just culture is a superior business model that differentiates companies through attributes that dramatically enable elevated organizational performance. Progressive discipline involves documentation and "strikes." The first strike might be a warning. The second might be suspension, etc. It is robotic, robbing managers of the ability to use their judgment. It also breeds mistrust and resentment among employees.

In contrast, a just culture is about facts, circumstances, and fairness. In most situations, documented coaching replaces discipline. It is a balanced business standard that provides a variety of benefits:

1. **Systemic accountability.** There should be accountability between designed management systems and the employees working inside those systems.

2. **Workplace dignity and justice with a purpose.** It demonstrates in real time that the senior management is committed to living up to organizational values.

3. **An employee-centric, values-supportive approach to customer service.** Most service initiatives place the customer as the principal focus. In this approach, excellent customer experience is a by-product of engaged employees working inside well-designed systems.

4. **A coherent approach to operational performance improvement initiatives.** This optimizes return on investment through enterprise alignment and balancing competing business priorities in safety, human resources, risk, and logistics.

5. **Improved labor relations and worker satisfaction.** Employees are respected as partners in achieving strategic alignment and stronger operational performance.

In my company, we began looking at a failure as either reckless behavior or an honest mistake. If we see that the employee demonstrated reckless behavior, then, of course, the severity of the action or offense requires consequences. It is critical that employees know what behaviors will generate this type of action. Swift action must be taken for gross violations of your core company values. For example, our team created the "Serious Six," which includes speeding or using a handheld device while driving. Those are the rules that, when violated, could kill or seriously harm the employee or a member of the public. For violations such as this, many times the "one strike, and you're out" mentality is the fair and just guiding force in a decision.

If we determine that an error is the result of an honest mistake, then coaching takes precedence over formal discipline. In a culture where fairness rules, decisions are made looking at all relevant factors as a whole: seniority, performance, attitude, behavior, and other relevant considerations. Careful thought is given to each area.

Practicing the tool of organizational accountability also can help shed light on contributing factors to what happened and identify any policies or procedures that need changing or updating to help ensure that similar problems and mistakes won't be repeated. The finger of blame is not frozen in the path of one individual.

The goal of leaders in a vibrant culture is for employees to know they will be treated fairly in any situation. Since moving to a "just culture" HR system, we've seen employee turnover decrease, and accountability increase. By steering away from a rigid, rule-bound method of treating your employees and operating with a broader sense of fairness and justice, trust will grow. As trust grows, your bond with your employees also will blossom.

CHAPTER 3: RESPONSIBILITY
TAKEAWAYS AND TIPS

- Ask your team or organization how you are performing respective to this dimension: In a company that values responsibility, people are accountable for their actions and have the independence to make decisions regarding their work. How would you rate responsibility at your organization?

- Involve employees in workplace decisions, such as naming the conference rooms and choosing the office snacks.

- Allow employees to decorate their workspace.

- Create committees that employees of all levels can participate in, such as an office beautification committee.

- Encourage leaders to coach rather than jump in with solutions when supporting their direct reports.

- Create clear decision-making criteria for projects. If there are certain organizational priorities that everyone should consider, share those as well.

- Before launching projects, have teams identify who and what will be impacted by the deliverables.

- Create a process for recording action items after meetings and in emails.

CHAPTER 4:

AGILITY

BY NOW WE KNOW THAT CHANGE—IN THE MARKET, WITHIN YOUR COMPANY, ON YOUR TEAMS—IS CONSTANT AND INEVITABLE, AND IT'S CERTAINLY NOT SLOWING DOWN ANY TIME SOON.

How your organization reacts to that inevitably affects your employees and your business. As famous educator Peter Drucker wrote, "The greatest danger in times of turbulence is not the turbulence—it is to act with yesterday's logic."

This brings us to the natural question: How do we act with today's logic? Today's logic requires a fundamental shift in how we operate. My favorite analogy to explain this comes from McKinsey. An internal group of fifty cross-functional colleagues, known as the McKinsey Agile Tribe, calls for thinking of organizations as living organisms rather than as machines.[33] A machine can move quickly, but if the surrounding environment changes too drastically or frequently, its stability often suffers. Meanwhile, maintaining stability and dynamism within an ever-changing environment is core to an organism's survival.

That adaptability is what agility is all about. Research shows us just how important adapting to these forces is for your company's success.

Analyzing agility and financial data from sixty-one Fortune 500 companies, the data team at CultureIQ demonstrated that agility dramatically impacts financial results. We found that profit margins were percentage points higher for organizations that scored in the top quartile when measuring agility versus companies that scored in the bottom quartile when measuring agility. This sizable difference is evidence that agility is a competitive advantage.

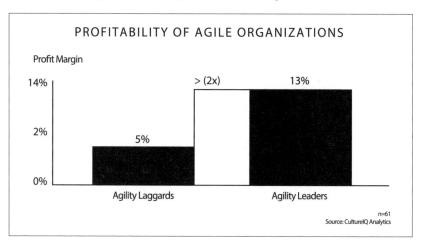

PROFITABILITY OF AGILE ORGANIZATIONS

The goal of this chapter is to help you, as a business leader, make your organization more like a living organism than a machine by exploring ways to foster agility. Air travel often frustrates consumers, and airlines are not typically confused with a living organism. When it comes to embracing a corporate culture that is agile and engaging though, many experts point to Southwest Airlines. Air Canada is another leader in making a radical and profitable commitment to culture.

"Even though Air Canada was over eighty years old," writes Fauzia Sikender, manager of employee engagement, "we referred to ourselves as an eighty-year-old start-up. Our mindsets were shifting from the traditional hierarchical model toward a more horizontal one.

"We wanted to empower our employees by giving them a voice, hearing what they said, and responding to their needs. The engagement survey allowed us to do that, and it was the perfect medium to communicate with them globally.

"Even though we knew agility, collaboration, and communication were three cultural dimensions linked to preparing employees for the future, we decided to focus on wellness, support, and work environment after receiving the results from the survey.

"Some branches held gatherings with their teams, implemented interactive exercises, and came up with action plans based on their employee feedback. Other branches offered soft skill training to empower their employees when handling conflicts or dealing with challenging situations.

"As a result, we started to build a more strongly engaged workforce and were able to reinforce agility, communication, and collaboration with our WIN as ONE approach. Because these dimensions are key to staying connected. And when we stay connected to one another and focus on a common goal, we can do anything.

"Therefore, to prepare ourselves for the inevitable change that the future brings with it, we strengthened the layers of our foundation, increased our employee engagement, and offered support and training. Today, we are implementing change management initiatives that include training to continuously support our employees while we introduce new technologies and AI initiatives in our workplace."

That is exactly what an agile organization looks like!

Agility is the ability to quickly respond and adapt to opportunities as they arise. Within an agile organization, managers and individual contributors have an open mindset and remain flexible in their roles.

They consistently learn from previous experiences to improve upon the status quo.

What makes agility more important than ever before is that opportunities are always arising, given the changing nature of the future of work. We often think of technology as being the primary force in how the workplace is changing, but that is just the tip of the iceberg.

Six forces are shaping the future of work, according to researchers at Harvard Business School and the Boston Consulting Group's Henderson Institute.[34] They are:

1. Accelerating technological change that has the potential to supplement or replace human labor.

2. Growing demand for skills for current roles and evolving jobs.

3. Changing employee expectations around employer/employee relations.

4. Shifting labor demographics and the need to provide opportunities for underrepresented populations.

5. Transitioning work models, such as freelancing, remote, and partner ecosystems.

6. Evolving business environment that includes new regulations and political volatility.

How is one to keep up with these? I've identified four keys to anticipating what organizations need to do in the future and will walk you through them in this chapter.

1. Normalize ambiguity.

2. Embrace an agile mindset.

3. Prepare employees for the future through learning and development.

4. Continuously monitor and respond.

NORMALIZE AMBIGUITY

In tennis, you start every point with a split step—on your toes, knees slightly bent, ready to move in any direction because you never know where your opponent will hit the ball next. Tennis players don't feel as if something is wrong because they're not sure what's to come; instead, they know this is part of playing the game. In fact, it's what makes the game challenging and fun!

This is like normalizing ambiguity in your organization: accepting that the future is unpredictable and creating norms so that employees feel stable and prepared regardless. The difference between working amid ambiguity and normalizing it is setting expectations accordingly.

These days ambiguity is a reality among companies old and new. People who accept that business affairs will always be in a state of flux are more likely to embrace agile mindsets. People who don't like change and don't want to learn will have a hard time in agile cultures.

EMBRACE AGILE MINDSETS

Three mindsets support agility, according to the article *Viewpoint: How to Develop an Agile Workforce,*[35] by Ryan Gottfredson, a leadership consultant and professor at California State University, Fullerton. They are: a growth mindset, an open mindset, and a promotion mindset.

A growth mindset, as opposed to a fixed mindset, is the belief that one can improve and develop personal abilities. This concept was developed by Carol Dweck, a psychology professor at Stanford University. In her TED talk, she shares how she was inspired to explore this idea after learning of a Chicago school that referred to non-passing grades as "Not Yet," reframing something usually regarded as failure into a learning journey with a path to the future.[36]

You can see how a growth mindset encourages people to try new things and treat experiences as learning opportunities. What's more, Dweck's research found that when entire companies embrace a growth mindset, their employees feel more committed and supported when compared with those who have a fixed mindset.[37]

An open mindset, versus a closed mindset, is one's willingness to listen to and learn from other perspectives. When you seek out new perspectives, you're more likely to identify unique opportunities for improvement that you might have missed. This mindset primes you to learn from and accept feedback from peers, direct reports, and clients alike. As a leader, it's particularly important for you to model this approach so that employees view feedback and diversity of thought as a positive contribution to the company.

Michael Kiolbassa, the president of Kiolbassa Smoked Meats, shows the potential you can unlock—in yourself, in your company, and in your business—if you embrace feedback, new perspectives, and the willingness to change. You can read more in our feature culture story.

Finally, you want to have a promotional, proactive mindset, focused on advancing and improving rather than "not losing." Agility is about being can-do and flexible; it's about leaning into the challenge. This encourages prioritization and healthy risk-taking. House of Kaizen incorporates this mindset in the company's name: Kaizen is a Japanese business philosophy that centers on continuous improvement.[38]

As Matt Cronin, founding partner of House of Kaizen, explains, after the digital marketing agency managed to survive the 2008 economic recession, the company was stagnating and needed to reflect and refocus.

"It was at this time that we decided to reinterview each of our staff members in offices in New York City and London. We sought to understand what gets them out of bed each day, what 'fills up their cup,' and how their work contributes to their broader life plans. Through this process we began to evolve our culture into a community.

"Rather than assuming that the values of the founders can be imposed upon the team, we embraced the values of our team and made it a priority to support and elevate those. We had done a great job of hiring good people, but it wasn't until embracing this perspective that we were able to really empower them to be their best in life and at work.

"Achieving this outcome required reprioritizing our time and the amount of it we allow our team to invest in themselves. From there it became easy to implement programs and policies that directly improved our workplace and our team members' lives. For one, we quickly dispelled the false value of face time by giving individuals lots of autonomy with their work schedules and their location. We now emphasize responsibility and evaluate performance and productivity on specific contributions, not hours in the office.

"By giving our team more of their most valuable asset, time, we immediately saw improvements in the amount and quality of our work as well as the satisfaction of those doing it. Further, we invested in services that can ease everyone's efficiency at work and at home; we provide apps for health care advice, subscriptions to valued products and services, and full benefits to part-time employees who wish to balance their personal interests alongside their profession."

Of course, organizations need to incentivize agile thinking by hiring, rewarding, training, and modeling accordingly. You can build organizational systems that help employees flex their agile mindsets. Digital publisher Twinkl's process of "black box" thinking provides a great example of this in action. After every project, Twinkl employees ask themselves and each other: "What went well? What could have been improved? What was unexpected? What next?"

MEASURING AND OPTIMIZING CULTURE

Agility is also about proactively identifying opportunities to optimize. When it comes to most areas of business, such as sales, marketing, and product, leaders of most companies rely on data that we collect and monitor to provide insights.

I call this culture management, and it is a key part of maintaining an agile culture. In the same way you measure whether your marketing campaigns are effective and adjust accordingly, you should assess your culture so you know how to direct your efforts.

Historically, organizations have collected employee feedback either once a year or not at all. However, think about how much can change within a year or even a month! We need shorter feedback and response loops to stay agile. I recommend crafting systems for employees to provide regular feedback about both specific initiatives and their broader experience within the organization. CultureIQ uses what we call an "employee listening" program as a key component of human resources analytics efforts. An employee listening program should include a variety of channels, including:

- Culture and engagement surveys: Comprehensive employee surveys that measure key metrics on evergreen topics such as mission alignment, agility, and engagement. They provide an overview of the state of your culture to help you identify areas of focus. Many organizations use culture and engagement surveys to establish a baseline to compare results from year to year. Topics remain consistent, so your leadership can make meaningful comparisons of the data.

- Pulse surveys: Shorter, more frequent employee surveys that can help you understand how employees perceive specific concepts and initiatives, assess how your efforts are performing, and collect suggestions from your employees.

- Focus groups: Voluntary focus groups can provide more qualitative and anecdotal feedback on initiatives or change efforts.

- Onboarding and exit interviews or surveys: These interviews are conducted to understand why an employee joins your organization (onboarding) and why an employee leaves (exit).

After collecting the feedback, acknowledge it and respond. Employees will know that you listen and care about their feedback. Explain what you have found, and be transparent about the findings. Then promote the distinct changes, initiatives, or programs that employees can expect to see in the near future. Further, ensure that leaders across levels are equipped with the data relevant to their scopes of control. Finally, as you launch projects throughout the year, mention whether the employee feedback informed the planning behind any of these projects.

What I love most about this process is that it embodies the three agile mindsets—growth, open, and performance—mentioned in the previous section. Being transparent about the iterative and learning process can have a powerful impact on employee buy-in. Explain to employees that you are all in this together, even if you can't immediately address everything noted in the feedback. A significant benefit of active culture management is that employees see that you care. They see that culture is not static, that they have input, and that if they are unhappy with a certain aspect, they have the power to help affect positive change.

CREATING A SOPHISTICATED HR ANALYTICS PROGRAM

Developing a program of research and analytics to yield insights rarely happens overnight. However, with the rapid evolution of HR metrics and the need to base concrete decisions and actions on data, the expectations to build an effective program remain high. To take the right steps, here are some best practices:

- Analytics is first and foremost about behavior change. Ensure that your analyses focus on solving critical problems by asking your stakeholders the right questions. Only then will the analyses be strategic and insightful.

- Analytics requires change management. Effectively communicating and translating the findings of analyses into action takes time, planning, and some education.

- Analytics is about application, not just understanding. Developing prescriptive guidance for your stakeholders based on the evidence will go a long way toward building the credibility of the analytics program.

- Analytics is never one-and-done. The answers to questions involving human behavior are rarely straightforward. Often multiple iterations and testing of assumptions are required to reach a high level of confidence in the conclusions.

- Analytics rarely provides a one-size-fits-all solution. While many similarities exist, employee populations are diverse, and the best predictive models will take diversity into consideration. This consideration will allow better translation of insights into actions that are more precise and localized.

PREPARE EMPLOYEES THROUGH LEARNING AND DEVELOPMENT

Managing change within an organization is often challenging, but the good news is that the overwhelming majority of employees want to learn, develop, and grow with your company. A survey of thousands of business leaders and workers by Harvard Business School and the Boston Consulting Group found that workers are far more optimistic about and adaptable to change than their leaders think. They just want more support doing it![39]

One of the best ways to prepare employees for the future is to support their development through training programs. Not only does providing training demonstrate an organizational commitment to a growth mindset, but also it equips employees with the skills needed to evolve with the company. House of Kaizen recognizes the importance of this and dedicates 25 percent of its time to employee development.

Remember the model of viewing organizations as organisms rather than machines and maintaining both dynamism and stability for survival? Well, learning and development programs are necessary to provide employees with the skills and knowledge fundamental to their roles now (stability) and those of the future (dynamism). Kiolbassa, in the example that follows, prioritized manager training during its culture change journey. If managers feel confident in their roles, they will be better able to weather change and lead their teams through to new business landscapes. Air Canada also leverages training to prepare employees for the future. In addition to training in soft skills such as resolving conflicts and managing challenging situations, the airline offers training in building employee confidence as new technologies are introduced.

FEATURE STORY
AGILITY

Kiolbassa: What a Journey It Has Been

By Michael Kiolbassa, President

"Are you kidding me? I am completely conscious of all of my commitments!" I answered as Jim, the consultant I had brought in to lead my YPO (Young Presidents' Organization, a global CEO peer group) chapter retreat, asked members to write down an unconscious commitment that we had. Psychobabble, I thought. But fear was what was really going through my mind. In my attempt to resuscitate my YPO chapter's engagement level with each other, I was really in the process of resuscitating my own ability to look hard at myself and my leadership of my family company.

I am the third generation to lead my family's meat packing and sausage manufacturing company, founded in San Antonio, Texas, and we all know the statistics surrounding the success of the third generation... not good. But for twenty-two years, I had grown the company significantly, successfully shifting our focus from a commodity-driven cattle and hog slaughtering operation to a value-added branded sausage company that was well -regarded in our industry for quality and service. I grew the value of the enterprise and successfully managed the dynamics of a father-son working relationship. But there was something wrong, and Jim was probing hard. When I called "bullshit" on his question, he looked at me and said, "Michael, you have a lot of unconscious commitments!" And he was right.

So I dug deep and came up with one. I wrote down that I have an unconscious commitment to have my finger in every part of our business. I love to micromanage. He said, "Good, that's a good one! Now, how do you live out your UCC?"

I said, "Well, I am the sales manager; I buy all of the raw materials for our products; I set up all of the promotions; I get involved when production issues come up; and I basically don't trust others to get things right."

"Great," Jim responded. "How does your UCC serve you?"

"Well, it makes me feel like I'm in control. It makes me feel like I am earning my paycheck. After all, this is mine and my family's largest asset, and I need to know what is going on in all the areas of the company!"

"Great," Jim replied again. "Now the question that I really want you to think about: Is it working for you?"

Wow. What a great question to ask someone. Was it working for me? Absolutely not! I was stressed. Our bottom line was not growing as fast as our top line. We were not achieving our potential. From a personal level, I know that I wasn't being the best husband or father because of the stress, and I hadn't slept well in a long time.

Jim asked me, "What's at risk if you change?"

I replied, "Well, loss of control, loss of power and prestige within the company, loss of income. If we don't execute well, temporary frustration as people learn the things that I already knew."

He said, "OK. Are you willing to change?" As the clarity around how foolish I had been hit me square in the face, I said, "Yes. I am willing to change."

What made this conversation and exercise with Jim so annoying was that I am, at heart, a culture geek. It started when I was in college, and my favorite business school class was *Organizational Behavior and Management*. I loved how the dynamics of an organization help make it successful.

When I made the move to join our family company in 1987, culture was one of my primary focal points. My father was a hard-working and very capable leader of our company. He had been forced into leadership when my grandfather, the founder of our company, became sick with a brain tumor and died at the age of 45. That was 1958, and my father dropped out of college to run the business. It wasn't necessarily what he had in mind for a career, but he did an amazing job of keeping the business going and growing it significantly. He led by example, and his employees respected him greatly. When he expanded our operation into cattle and hog slaughtering in the late 1970s, the business became more complex and difficult to manage. However, he was conservative from a financial perspective and successfully weathered every storm that came his way. He valued people, and they valued him.

As our business grew, I took on more responsibilities, and I became president of the company in 1999. I still focused primarily on growth and not on culture. I tried to spend time with employees as much as I could, but my travel schedule really did not permit the kind of time that it takes to develop deep relationships. In 2002 I hired our first significant non-family employee since 1977, an engineer who quickly became an important operations manager. He had an impressive resume from larger companies, some of which had great cultures, and we would talk … just talk … about how important culture was to a company's success.

Like many sons in family businesses, I took on my father's work ethic, and as we grew, I worked harder and harder. I was always the sales manager, but when my father had heart bypass surgery in 2005, I took on additional roles in the company. Again, although I knew the importance of culture in the success of a business, I simply did not have the time to focus on it. Or I should say that I decided to focus on the tasks of our business instead of our people.

Fast-forward 13 months later to my exercise to name my unconscious commitment with Jim at our YPO chapter retreat. After my answer that I was ready for change, Jim walked me through a set of action plans designed to break through my fears and to offload all the tasks that I had acquired over the years. I was so emotionally exhausted after our meeting that I took a three-hour nap before I drove home.

On the drive, I committed emotionally to the action plans on which we had worked, which was a crucial commitment for me. The next day, I met with all my direct reports and gave them their new assignments. Without any exceptions, each one of them was grateful and eager to take on the responsibility. The engineer I hired back in 2002 even told me, "Michael, it's about time!"

The next year we had another chapter retreat, and Jim was there again. He asked how things were going, and I said, "Great!" We still had a lot of work to do, but my team was learning and growing. I was still focused on growth, but I was much happier. At the retreat we spent a lot of time talking about culture and our leadership to build a great culture. I left with a new conviction in the importance of culture. I saw so many missed opportunities in our company and came back from that retreat committed to focusing on culture!

I also committed at that retreat to hire a strong vice president of sales (whom I had been courting for several months) and an HR manager. This would allow me to have the time and energy to focus on refining our culture. Six months later, in February 2012, I hired a 25-year veteran of the largest protein company in the world to be our VP of sales. In the same month, I hired a veteran HR manager to build our HR systems and processes in line with my cultural vision for our company.

That month, I began to take individual employees out to lunch so that I could get to know them better. These were line employees, and some couldn't speak English, so I would take our HR manager with me to translate. The lunches were meant for me to get to know them better and learn about their families, hobbies, and concerns, but the conversation would inevitably turn to business. A steady refrain from all the employees that I took to lunch was: "Hey, Michael, I love working for you, but my boss is an asshole!"

What I discovered is that, as we grew the company—we now had about ninety employees—we took high-performing machine operators and made them leads and supervisors without giving them any leadership training! Not very smart. In the summer of 2012, I began looking for a leadership development program that would help train our supervisors on how to lead.

Our HR manager suggested several companies and consultants that we could bring in to train our team. One of them was

Holt Development, the training arm of the Holt Companies, a diversified family-owned company whose primary assets are Caterpillar dealerships across the country and the San Antonio Spurs, a professional basketball team known for its successful culture. Their model of leadership development is values-based leadership (VBL), first developed by Ken Blanchard in the 1980s. I had actually come across Holt in the book *Managing by Values* twenty years earlier when I was reading about great company cultures, so it was familiar to me. It also happened to be the most expensive program that we were looking at, so I asked Holt if they could give me some references from companies who had invested in VBL, and I could find out firsthand how successful the program had been.

Holt suggested that I call Charlie Luck, the CEO of Luck Companies in Richmond, Virginia, to get an idea of not only the success of VBL in his company, but also the commitment that it will take to successfully integrate VBL into our culture. I researched Charlie and found out that he was a YPO-er, and I reached out to him for a phone call. When Charlie called back, the first thirty minutes of our call was an interrogation of me by Charlie to see if I was committed enough to take on VBL and invest in our culture. After I convinced him that I was, he invited me to Richmond to stay with him and his wife and meet his team to discuss the power of VBL in his organization. That was one of the best decisions I have ever made.

I came back from that trip convinced that if we were going to invest the time and money into a leadership development program, VBL was the only one that I wanted. We hired Holt to help us define our vision (why we exist), our mission (what we do), and our core values (how we do it). It took several months for us to nail these down because we wanted everyone in our organization to be involved in their development.

Because we had a good culture base to begin with, VBL took root fairly quickly. I know that this doesn't always happen, but we knew that we needed this and were ready for it. It has been easier for some of our team members than others. Charlie was right: It was very difficult at times to use, especially when we had been doing things differently for many years. We had some colorful discussions over tough people issues, but at the end of the day, we stayed focused on our vision, mission, and values.

What a journey it has been. If anyone thinks that culture is soft, they can think again. Our culture, centered on values-based leadership and teaching financial literacy through the Great Game of Business, has allowed us to continue our explosive growth, but now our bottom line is growing faster than our top line. We have found capacity within our plant that will allow us to continue our growth while building cash. Our team members are set to get their first bonus checks, and engagement has never been higher. We have initiated a Kiolbassa Business Leadership class that is developing a new generation of leaders of our company. I have never been more energized and more conscious of my "unconscious" commitments!

CHAPTER 4: AGILITY
TAKEAWAYS AND TIPS

- Ask your team or organization how you are performing respective to this dimension: A company with agility quickly responds and adapts to opportunities. How would you rate your organization's agility?

- Conduct a needs analysis to identify skill assessment gaps and then provide training accordingly.

- Screen for a growth mindset, open mindset, and performance mindset during interviews.

- Collect employee feedback to measure and monitor your culture.

- Collect feedback after key initiatives.

- Incorporate the norm of having retrospectives after each project and train project leads on conducting these retrospectives.

- Build out an HR dashboard including, but not limited to, data around your culture, retention, hiring, diversity, and employee sentiment.

CHAPTER 5:

WORK ENVIRONMENT

THE AVERAGE PERSON SPENDS NINETY THOUSAND HOURS AT WORK OVER THE COURSE OF A LIFETIME.[40] This could be a hint to why work environment surfaced as the top driver of engagement, as measured by employee Net Promoter Score, in a CultureIQ survey of nearly thirty thousand employees from more than three hundred companies.[41] This means that in the journey to improve employee engagement, tinkering with the environment of your office is a high-impact and accessible place to start.

DRIVER ANALYSIS - LINEAR REGRESSION

Thinking of great work environments brings images of the gorgeous campuses of Google, Apple, and the like to mind. And given the results illustrated above, it's no coincidence that these pioneers of employee experience have invested heavily in their physical work environment. However, this chapter will show that you don't need to be a giant technology company to create a work environment in which employee productivity and morale thrive.

I'm defining work environment as the physical space, surroundings, and resources that employees interact with at work. In effective work environments, employees feel safe and comfortable in their surroundings, are able to be productive in their workspaces, and have the resources to get work done.

The good news is that there is plenty of research outlining what physical factors drive productivity and performance. The companies with the best work environments not only follow those best practices, but also recognize that everything in one's work environment sends messages (intentionally and unintentionally) about what behaviors are accepted and what type of culture is promoted. The key is to create an environment that facilitates productivity, enhances morale, and aligns with your values as a company.

Below I explore a few factors to consider when shaping your work environment: layout, temperature, design, virtual environment, and alignment.

OFFICE LAYOUT

Consider, for example, open office spaces. They send a signal of transparency, collaboration, and a lack of hierarchy. However, as introvert advocate Susan Cain brought to our attention in her book *Quiet: The Power of Introverts in a World That Can't Stop Talking*,[42] open layouts are not suited for everyone's work style. In fact, a study published in the *Philosophical Transactions of the Royal Society*[43] found that face-to-face interaction actually decreased by 70 percent when employees shifted to an open floor plan from a traditional, partitioned one.

If your office, like two-thirds of offices in the United States (including mine), has an open floor plan, designate a small nook or corner in the office as a quiet space.[44] You can purchase free-standing dividers to physically separate the area. Employees can go here if they need to recharge from the chaos of an open floor plan.

Similarly, carving out a physical space for employees to momentarily step away from their desk signals that breaks are accepted and encouraged. These spaces also can help to refocus employees and keep energy levels high. If your office is short on space, a coffee or tea station could do the trick.

Given the welcomed diversity of work styles in any given office, it will be impossible to please everyone with a single setup. The key is to provide a variety of options so that individuals can craft the setup that works best for their needs at any given time.

TEMPERATURE

You might be asking yourself: Why am I reading about room temperature in a business book about organizational culture? In addition to affecting employees' comfort level, temperature also impacts output and productivity. Plus as business leaders, we face plenty of factors that feel out of our control, so it can be nice to focus on things that we can control.

The challenge is that we lack a solid consensus on the optimal office temperature. In 2004 researchers at Cornell University spent a month studying workers at an insurance company to understand the impact of temperature on productivity.[45] They found that when they raised the temperature from 68° to 77° Fahrenheit, typing errors dropped by 44 percent, and output increased by 150 percent. In 2006 the Lawrence Berkeley National Laboratory and the Helsinki University of Technology found that 22° Celsius, or 71.6° Fahrenheit, is the optimal temperature for worker productivity.[46] So where does that leave us in our hunt for the Goldilocks office temperature? Likely around 71.6°, but try to find the optimal range at your company.

DESIGN

Two companies wrote us culture stories about offices that are nestled in nature to inspire creativity and connection among employees. After all, it's no secret that our surroundings affect our mood and experience. My interest in citing these two examples lies not in suggesting that you're falling short in your life if your company lacks such options, but in showing the commitment of leaders to the role of work environment. These companies may inspire creative thinking of your own.

Mirego's Mirechalet, located in the Charlevoix mountains in Canada, has fifteen beds, three bathrooms, optimized work areas to accommodate the teams, a living room with a view of the mountains, a stable Internet connection, a coffee machine, a spacious shared kitchen, and much more.

According to the team at Mirego, the "Mirechalet serves two purposes: We go for intense work sessions, when a team needs to isolate themselves and work intensively on a project, and we use it for team celebrations, for instance, when a team ships an app they have been working on for a long time. We work hard together, so we think it's important to celebrate our successes together. Our culture is very much like a family. People appreciate spending time with their colleagues outside work, and the chalet solidifies this culture."

I appreciate how the Mirechalet idea grew organically from the company's passionate culture connection. "One of Mirego's key pillars is experimentation. We may not possess the key to infused science, but we do have a strong desire to innovate and reinvent conventions. The Mirechalet was born out of this spirit of experimentation. We first rented a chalet in the same area of Charlevoix, Québec, for few weeks in 2015. We took several teams for work retreats and fell in love with the vibe, the scenery, and the outcomes of these retreats. It allowed us to be very creative and productive.

"This experience inspired us to build our very own chalet for our team to use whenever they wanted. It serves as the ideal place for brainstorms and work blitzes. Who said you had to work behind a desk from 9 to 5 to be productive and get the job done? We sure didn't. With the right tools and proper processes, locational constraints become irrelevant."

The digital marketing firm GetUWired could have put its offices in a suburban office park in Atlanta, Georgia, but instead chose to rent a gorgeous cabin in the foothills of the Blue Ridge Mountains. The cabin isn't a gimmick; it is core to the vision of the agency's founders and a place where staff play Frisbee, jam with banjos, and eat at picnic tables. It's all about the commitment of the founders to putting people first.

According to copywriter Ella Wilson, the company "operates under a shared vision that we created as a team in 2014. Over two days and several boxes of doughnuts, the entire staff came up with a set of core values that truly reflects the spirit of GetUWired. Creating our vision as a team serves two purposes: to show the employees that their input is valued and to create core values that actually mean something to the staff—something we can actually live by.

"The leadership team goes out of its way to make sure employees feel appreciated, honored, and listened to. Our opinions matter. As we grow, they've been committed to making sure our culture stays the same no matter how many people we have. Other companies lose that as they grow, but we haven't. The leaders of our company proactively tackle the issue because they know how important our culture is to our company."

It's not about the cabin; it's about the culture.

If you, like me, are not able to move your offices to the middle of the woods, you still have plenty of opportunities to use design and color to inspire and engage your team. For one, you can bring nature inside your office. A study by the University of Queensland found that adding plants to your office can make employees happier and boost their concentration.[47] And that's not the only benefit plants bring to your workplace. They also bring a burst of color, which the field of environmental psychology tells us can influence our emotions.[48]

For example, a 2016 *Harvard Business Review* article by Sally Augustin shares that "we're relaxed in the presence of colors that aren't very saturated but are relatively bright and that aren't cluttered."[49] Decide what energy you want to convey in each room, and then choose your colors accordingly. Sure, you can repaint your walls, but you can be on the lookout for simple opportunities to intentionally add color to the space, such as colorful drawer sets, wall art, or even flowers.

WORKING FROM HOME

In this chapter we reviewed data revealing work environment as the top driver of employee engagement. Most data and examples represent those who work in a corporate setting, but what about employee engagement for those who work remotely?

Prior to the coronavirus pandemic, employees working remotely were already a growing trend. According to U.S. Census data, approximately five percent of employees in the United States worked at home in 2017. This percentage increased a whopping fifty-eight percent since 2000. However, until recently most organizations accommodated remote employees to solve for unique circumstances. Since these were often one-off situations, most organizations did not have company-wide policies, procedures, or infrastructure to support a large percentage of employees working remotely. The COVID-19 pandemic accelerated this remote work trend practically overnight, and it required almost every organization to rapidly implement thoughtful policies and procedures.

Since the future of work has arrived sooner than expected, how do you make sure that your remote employee guidelines become an important part of your formula to achieve a high-performance culture? What programs should leaders implement to make sure that employees working remotely are just as engaged as those working in a corporate office?

In response to this rapid acceleration of working remotely, CultureIQ created a resource called the Remote Work Guidance Center, which includes strategies and tips for remote employees. These recommended best practices were provided in response to the coronavirus, but they should be considered for any environment. One of the resources provided in the Remote Work Guidance Center is a thought leadership article titled *Eight Ways That Organizations Can Support Remote Work*[50] featured below.

WORK ENVIRONMENTS FOR DISTRIBUTED AND REMOTE TEAMS

In 2016, Gallup found that more than four in ten employees work away from their team members at least part of the time.[51] What happens if you don't have walls to hang art or conference rooms to put plants? How do you shape a virtual environment that enables the same type of team connection and collaboration as a physical office?

The chargeback management company Midigator, based in American Fork, Utah carves out digital space and time to connect remote employees and those from different regional offices. For example, the core operating hours are set from 10 a.m. to 4 p.m., which serve as "time walls" that people can interact within. The company also uses group chat to share photos of these workers participating in parallel activities.

Donco Recycling Solutions, headquartered in Chicago, uses what is typically wasted physical space for company-wide communication and illustrates the concept of productive reuse at the same time. This focal point is an erasable wall at the front of their bullpen. "The wall starts clean at the first of each month," relates CEO David Mendelson, "and throughout the next thirty days the team adds seasonal art, ideas, problems to be solved, solutions that have been created. At the end of the month, a picture is taken and distributed to the entire company, the wall is erased, and we start again. This simple dry-erase board has created a really neat way to engage the creative juices in our team and spread information in a more upbeat way than the standard two-page office memo."

ALIGNMENT

Remember that iceberg image in the About Culture chapter? Your work environment is the tip of the iceberg: a visible artifact of your company culture. It's a key opportunity to "walk the talk" and demonstrate what your organization prioritizes. For example, if there is dedicated space such as a soundproof conference room to freely express yourself and experiment, this indicates to your staff that the company values innovation.

The software company HoneyBook is a great example of workplace and value alignment. With the core value "People Come First," the staff designed their office to accommodate different work styles so people feel comfortable bringing their full selves to work. Plus they intentionally designed their office in Tel Aviv, Israel, to emulate their home office in San Francisco, which demonstrates that the two locations are equally important.

"People have always been at the heart of our office spaces," Allie Mintz, Director of People, writes. "In fact, the first HoneyBook office was in a cozy two-bedroom apartment in San Francisco. People showed up in their slippers and cooked breakfast every morning. When we outgrew the apartment, we wanted to maintain this special ambiance in our new office space. It was an environment people not only wanted to work in, but actually thrived in.

"The open and accessible floor plan of our current office space allows employees to take a break and work at a dining room table, in the kitchen, or even on our indoor 'deck,' No matter what your work style preference is, there is a space for you.

"In the spirit of maintaining connection, our Tel Aviv office space echoes the design of the San Francisco office. Our team feels at home wherever they're working. And so do our members. We invite members to stop by and co-work alongside us whenever they get the chance (and always encourage taking boomerang videos in our swing seats). We serve creative professionals so the space where we work has to be inspiring for both employees of HoneyBook and members who visit."

Involve employees in designing the office layout. Follow the lead of various companies that survey their workforce to source and vote on conference room names. This sends a clear signal that they value differing opinions and that everyone has a role in shaping the culture.

When it comes to work environment, I understand that naming conference rooms can feel trivial. However, the data paint a clear picture. These little things can add up to big returns on employee engagement. The Takeaways and Tips below give you some action steps to consider for your company.

FEATURE STORY
REMOTE EMPLOYEES

CultureIQ: Eight Ways That Organizations Can Support Remote Work

CultureIQ has worked with a number of organizations that, prior to the coronavirus outbreak, successfully made the transition from office-based to remote work. Here's a list of best practices we've compiled from them to help both workers and their companies keep a healthy culture, no matter where the employees are.

1. **Provide the right remote-work tools.** At a tactical level, organizations need to think about what tools and resources are critical for employees to do their jobs. Video conferencing software is one that immediately jumps to mind, but what about other software or systems? Can employees remotely access secure folders and drives? Can phone calls be forwarded or accessed remotely? Perhaps most importantly, do employees know whom to contact with issues?

2. **Stay connected.** Many of us are feeling incredibly isolated right now, and organizations can help to bridge that gap by consciously focusing on the way we collaborate with one another. Team meetings should continue, perhaps more frequently than before, to allow team members not only to share work challenges, but also to

share challenges specific to remote work (and hopefully solutions!) with one another. Encourage phone calls and video calls whenever possible.

3. **Managers: Don't keep your distance.** Just as teams need to stay connected, so do managers. They may need to check in more frequently with their teams. Related to point #6 below, managers should be not only asking about work, but also finding out how employees are doing generally. Are they stressed? Worried? Confused? Do they have what they need to succeed? Try to facilitate an open dialogue where employees feel safe sharing.

4. **Be flexible and understanding.** Many employees are now serving as full-time caretakers for children, pets, and relatives on top of working a full-time job. Recognize that work hours need to be more flexible, either beginning earlier or ending later, as we try to flex around new challenges in our home work environments. Whenever possible, organizations should focus on what is getting done rather than when it is getting done. Similarly, we need to be understanding of employees who have to step away for a few minutes to take care of family needs, when a dog barks or when a child interrupts a phone call. It's critical for organizations to understand that not everyone has a perfect remote-work environment.

5. **Re-evaluate your usual habits.** Similarly, businesses need to be flexible about disruptions to usual processes. Consider whether some processes can be suspended, exceptions can be made, or new ways of working can be

required on an interim basis. It's important for managers to communicate expectations clearly, especially as work needs and processes change. This can be a great way to make employees feel connected: get their ideas on how to accomplish work in this new environment.

6. **Support physical and mental health.** Though many people are able to pack up their desks and work from home, we shouldn't assume that they are doing so without worry or stress. In fact, the uncertainty and unending pace of change can be incredibly stressful for employees. It's critical to remind employees what resources are available to them (e.g., telemedicine, employee assistance programs, counseling, etc.) to help alleviate these concerns.

7. **Honest and thorough communication is critical.** As we're all more distant physically, we need our employers to keep us up to date not only on remote work plans, but also about changes to the business or strategy. Transparency is always key, but especially so right now. The communications we send, particularly those from our leaders, set the tone for our organization, so we should balance pragmatism with optimism. If we're unsure of something –for example, how long employees will be working at home – it's OK to admit that, but balance that with what we do know. Updates should be frequent and always honest.

8. **Find some bright spots.** Finally, even in trying and uncertain times, it's important to find bright spots for everyone to share. For example, we should continue to

recognize good work by both individuals and teams. We might consider how we can adapt our day-to-day routines to a remote environment: If you normally do Friday catered lunches as a team, perhaps you can hold team lunches over video conference. Messaging tools can be fun ways for teams to stay connected. Just today, our colleagues at CultureIQ have been soliciting recommendations for TV shows and movies to watch as we practice our social distancing. (*Goodfellas, The Crown, The X Files, and Shaun the Sheep: Farmageddon* made the list.) Small actions like these can help to bolster morale and keep everyone connected and engaged.

CHAPTER 5: WORK ENVIRONMENT

TAKEAWAYS AND TIPS

- Ask your team or organization how you are performing respective to this dimension: A company with a great work environment has a comfortable workplace where people have the resources to be effective in their work. How would you rate your organization's work environment?

- Conduct a workplace audit:

  - List the different spaces in your office.

  - Observe how they are being used over a three-month period.

  - Challenge yourself to consider what signals your office layout is sending.

  - Ask employees with different work styles if there is a type of space they crave.

  - Consider policies and procedures for employees working remotely.

  - Review tools available for employees working remotely.

- Visit satellite offices to understand the experience of working there. Are any resources missing? Is it less or more comfortable? Whatever adjustments you make for yourself while there, consider implementing those in a systematic way throughout your company.

- Create a volunteer office beautification committee with a budget to experiment with ways to improve the workplace.

- Create a virtual space for people to connect, and set clear expectations for its use. Some examples include a Slack channel, Microsoft Teams, an opt-in email thread, or intranet.

- Play with hints of color and plants in the office.

- Carve out a quiet zone and develop a system to enforce that it is being used accordingly. Alternatively, explore a work-from-home policy for those who need quiet time.

- Create a space for employees to step away from their desk. This can be a couch, a tea cart, or a lunch table.

- Follow Donco's lead and dedicate space in the office that folks can contribute to or co-create. Not only does this instill a sense of ownership for employees, but also you never know what good ideas will be born from the process.

CHAPTER 6:

INNOVATION

*I*NNOVATION IS A CULTURE DIMENSION NEAR AND DEAR TO MY ENTREPRENEURIAL HEART. Innovation is essential to staying competitive in the market, meeting customer needs, increasing internal efficiency, and attracting top talent. Leaders also recognize that to reap the benefits of innovation, you must embrace a culture in which ideas can form, spread, and succeed.

When speaking with leaders, I find it helpful to focus on two key components of an innovative culture: first, an environment that promotes new ideas, and second, employees' ability to implement these ideas within the organization. I emphasize two components because one without the other is like bread that doesn't rise: all the ingredients are in place, but they're missing a crucial interaction. Let's explore these in more detail.

THE ENVIRONMENT

An environment that encourages new ideas isn't so much a physical space or a defined event, but rather a combination of conditions that encourage employees to generate and share new ideas.

Researchers at MIT Sloan School of Management call this "adaptive space."[52] After a decade of research and more than four hundred interviews, these researchers determined that the most successful innovations occur when companies have "the network and organizational context that allows people, ideas, information, and resources to flow across the organization." They do this by crafting "environments that open up information flows and enrich idea discovery, development, and amplification."

This concept highlights how innovation hinges on effective communication channels and a degree of transparency. For details, check out Chapter 2: Communication. Employees first must be aware of any current or potential challenges to inspire innovative ideas. They also need to have access to innovation success stories and understand the rationale behind why certain ideas are pursued over others. This could take place in company and team meetings, memos from leaders, and most important, informal and formal interactions with colleagues.

This brings me to my next point: Innovation relies on social interactions at work. The MIT Sloan research about adaptive space highlights the social nature of innovation and explains the importance of facilitating, understanding, and leveraging employee networks. Specifically, the researchers identified three network roles: brokers, central connectors, and energizers. Brokers are the liaisons from one group to another, ensuring that ideas are spread early and often. Central connectors organize their subgroups to see an idea through implementation. Energizers are highly influential people who inspire others to act and think boldly, with a contagious effect throughout the organization.

The main takeaway here is to consider how you as a leader are empowering people to fill their roles and creating space for these network interactions to take place. The innovation factories at history-defining companies such as Bell Labs at AT&T, Apple, and

Pixar, as well as at the National Aeronautics and Space Administration (NASA) and the weapons laboratories in World War II, all were characterized not by geniuses sitting alone in ivory towers, but by intellectuals having intense collaborations. At Apple, Steve Jobs was an energizer. At Los Alamos National Laboratory, it was Robert Oppenheimer.

My friend Tony Hsieh, CEO of Zappos, facilitates employee networks by promoting "culture collisions." In everything from the spatial nudges to work policies, Zappos encourages serendipitous encounters among employees. For example, the office is intentionally designed to funnel employees from different departments through specific spaces. Even if they don't interact in their day-to-day job, they inevitably will interact and share some insights about their work at the proverbial water cooler. The idea is that these culture collisions encourage collaboration, for example, when every single employee at Zappos, including Tony, jumps in to help with customer service during the busy holiday season. This exposes everyone to current processes and increases the chances of coming up with innovative ways to approach existing problems.

Finally and famously, innovative companies encourage experimentation and support learning from potential failures. Enter the Silicon Valley tagline: "Fail fast. Fail often." In practice, this means that in addition to sharing success stories, you should share unsuccessful attempts at innovation. You can call these "failure success stories," that is, failures from which you can learn and grow. Siren Design Group, with sites in Australia and across Asia, embeds this norm into its culture with a weekly reflection time, in which leaders and individual contributors alike share the lessons they learned that week.

As CEO Mia Feasey relates, "A lot of our success can be attributed to empowering our people to utilize their talents to bring these ideas to life. We like to think of it as leading from behind. There's a strong focus on paying it forward and nurturing our graduates instead of pigeon-holing them, encouraging that fresh talent to grow, be brave, and take risks. No hiding your light under a bushel here!"

Another way to do this is have postmortems after every project. What worked? What didn't? How can you learn from it? This will begin to normalize the sharing of failures and condition people to extract learning from them.

However, it's important to note that this tolerance for failure succeeds only when you have a foundation of standards for high performance.

"And yet for all their focus on tolerance for failure, innovative organizations are intolerant of incompetence. They set exceptionally high performance standards for their people. They recruit the best talent they can. Exploring risky ideas that ultimately fail is fine, but mediocre technical skills, sloppy thinking, bad work habits, and poor management are not," observes Gary P. Pisano of Harvard Business School in his 2019 HBR article *The Hard Truth About Innovative Cultures*.[53] This means you must have the right hiring standards, accountability measures, and behavioral expectations in place. For more on this topic, refer to Chapter 8: Performance Orientation.

THE PROCESSES

Once you have the foundation of an innovation-friendly environment, you can layer on the processes and formal programs that enable employees to implement new ideas. According to data from the hundreds of companies that participated in CultureIQ's Top Company Cultures,[54] nearly nine in ten respondents said that their company encourages new ideas; however, only seven in ten respondents understood the process for advancing new ideas. This means it's not the absence of new ideas that prevents companies from reaching their innovation potential; it's often the inability to push those ideas through the organization.

To prevent this common scenario, consider the following:

- Do employees know where to bring an idea when they have one?

- Do they have the skills to communicate new ideas, influence accordingly, and drive change?

- Do employees have the time, space, and budget to experiment?

This experimentation can take the form of a program or an event, such as company-wide hackathons. Inspira Marketing in Norwalk, Connecticut, has an annual "Big Ideas" contest in which teams generate innovative ways to have a positive impact on the community and propose them in a *Shark Tank*-type competition to the leadership team. What makes this so successful is that a formal space, time, and budget are set aside to execute on the winning idea as an entire company. This is a great example of how innovation requires intention, as you will see in Inspira's feature culture story.

At American Group real estate investments, Chairperson Fred Hameetman is the driving force behind a series of monthly lectures presented by select individuals with a proven track record in their field.

"Since 2007, our employees have heard from one of the top twenty scientists in the United States, a professional ukulele player, a CIA agent, a group of senior portfolio managers at a global investment firm, a principal architect, the chief of clinical nutrition and wellness at one of the top hospitals in the country, and many more," Hameetman explains. "In today's sharing economy, we share our cars, our homes, even our clothes. But perhaps the most important 'commodity' to be shared since humans learned to speak is knowledge."

Ernest Packaging Solutions, headquartered in Los Angeles, began as a paper company in 1946. In the words of CEO Tim Wilson, two brothers who had served in World War II started the company "selling boxes out of a garage in Los Angeles." Ernie and Chuck Wilson began building something great: "Over the next several decades, the duo continued to grow the business at a steady pace while retaining an extended family feeling within both the employee and leadership ranks."

As we have seen with other companies we studied, expansion and mergers created a culture crisis. According to Tim Wilson, "The late 1990s through 2008 marked a significant period of growth for Ernest, both in technological advances and the expansion across the United States. During this time, the company made more than thirty acquisitions, amounting to over one per year.

"The business now spans twelve locations nationwide, and we are over $250 million in sales. This roll-up strategy created a very frustrating climate as we acquired family businesses that had their own culture. Blending them into Ernest and pushing our culture on them did not work. We had to find a different way, a more innovative solution to get back to the values instilled by Ernie and Chuck. A solution that truly made the employees the keepers of the culture. A forum where everyone could speak and be heard, honestly and candidly. A place where geographical distances were irrelevant, where communication was simple, and where voices were heard from the employees up, as well as from the executive team down. Enter the Ernest Brand Council, known inside Ernest as the EBC.

"What began as the brainchild of Tim Wilson in 2011 soon turned into a driving force for unity across the entire company. Spearheaded by longtime employee Linda Rodriguez, the council's first chairwoman and "foremother," the EBC is a team of passionate individuals who are truly the keepers of Ernest culture. With twenty-six volunteers representing every division and every position, each serving for two years, this group is not only the eyes and ears of what's going on within Ernest. They're the voice of innovation, a driving force for improving processes, champions of employee recognition, and true leaders in employee involvement."

As part of this EBC, Ernest created an "ideation committee" dedicated to streamlining and driving business improvement ideas from all levels of the company. And the best part? The committee itself was born out of a formalized culture collision created by the leaders of Ernest. I bet that if I asked any employee at Ernest Packaging Solutions about when was the last time an employee's idea was implemented and where do employees go if they have a process improvement idea, they would be able to answer both questions easily. That is innovation at work.

FEATURE STORY
INNOVATION

Inspira Marketing: Big Ideas to Big Impact

By Jeff Snyder, Founder and CEO

I spent the first two decades of my career at leading experiential marketing agencies and was growing increasingly frustrated by what I saw. Agencies were drowning in a sea of sameness with no clear differentiator in terms of products and service, and there was a growing emphasis on the bottom line. Consequently, this was having an adverse effect on both the quality of work and employee morale. I believed I could do better.

I envisioned an agency built upon relationships and doing the right thing, where people would come before profits, where the team was passionate about the work they were doing (and had fun doing it!), and where optimism, innovation, and excellence ruled.

But my vision had to be put on hold. At the time, my then-two-year-old daughter, Kennedy, had just been diagnosed with a rare form of spinal cancer, and I was conscious of the consequences of losing health insurance and a guaranteed income at a critical time. But as she faced this life-threatening illness and rounds of chemotherapy treatments, I was in awe of her ability to approach any obstacle with optimism and tenacity. Her unwavering spirit inspired me to launch Inspira in 2008.

Most companies are lucky to have a clear mission, let alone a reason for being. With Kennedy as my inspiration, I placed living and working with passion and purpose at the heart of Inspira's philosophy. More important, I put my ideals into action by donating a portion of our profits to childhood cancer research and committing to providing ongoing pro bono marketing and creative work for Alex's Lemonade Stand Foundation for Childhood Cancer (ALSF).

When people are driven by a higher purpose, this creates an ecosystem fueled by passion and innovation. I hoped Inspira's purpose-driven culture would attract amazingly talented people who would thrive in our community, produce extraordinary work for our clients, and inspire people to act. And you know what? It worked.

A decade later, Inspira is thriving. We employ over four hundred fifty of arguably the best and brightest talent in the business with offices in Connecticut, New York City, and Chicago. Our client roster includes some of the world's most recognizable brands, many of whom have been with us since the beginning, and we are consistently recognized among the Top Places to Work. I attribute our success to our culture of putting people, passion, and purpose foremost in what we do and how we do it: for our business, for our clients, and in the lives of the people we touch through our activations.

Through our purpose-driven culture, Inspira has helped raise well over $1 million for pediatric cancer research through Alex's Lemonade Stand Foundation (ALSF), and our team actively participates in marquee events including Alex's Million Mile, the Chance for Life poker tournament, and Lemon: NYC.

What started with ALSF has taken on a life of its own. Although as a company we remain committed to ALSF, our commitment to creating an environment where people find purpose in their work has empowered our employees to take ownership of the company's culture and bring it to places I never expected.

Nowhere is this more evident than our annual "Big Idea" project. Each year our employees are divided into teams, and each team selects a local charity and collaborates to create an experiential program that they believe will have an overwhelmingly positive impact on the community. In *Shark Tank* fashion, each team presents its "Big Idea" to leadership, where two ideas are selected and put to a company-wide vote. The winning idea is then underwritten by Inspira and wholly executed by the entire company.

Our team pours its collective knowledge, experience, and expertise into these events. And it's not just limited to our current staff. Clients and even former employees come out to donate their time on a weekend to make a difference. Whether it's a day of giving, festively decorating the hospital rooms of sick children, coordinating a 4-Legged 4K to raise funds for a local animal shelter, or handing out backpacks filled with school supplies to children in underserved communities, the spirit of giving is woven into everything that we do. It's who we are. This is what I'm most proud of.

Our commitment to creating an environment where people find purpose in their work has fueled a unique culture that allows employees to pursue their own passions and feel fulfilled in a way that far exceeds the value of their paycheck. And the most glowing endorsement of all? People from outside of Inspira want to be a part of our culture, too, as evidenced by the constant flow of emails in my inbox from people dissatisfied with their current jobs and wanting to be a part of something bigger.

CHAPTER 6: INNNOVATION

TAKEAWAYS AND TIPS

- Ask your team or organization how you are performing respective to this dimension: An innovative company encourages new ideas and is able to move ideas through the organization. How would you rate your organization's innovation?

- Determine a process for sharing challenges, innovation success stories, and failure success stories.

- Create dedicated space and time for experimentation, such as hosting a hackathon or carving out a portion of everyone's role for passion projects.

- Identify your brokers, central connectors, and energizers. Ask yourself: Do they have the resources they need to thrive?

- Craft "culture collisions" of ideas and people, such as cross-functional committees, projects, and events.

- Set aside an experimentation budget for each team.

CHAPTER 7:

WELLNESS

PICTURE THIS: YOUR ORGANIZATION HAS WORKED HARD TO RECRUIT AND RETAIN THE TOP TALENT IN YOUR INDUSTRY. These employees are engaging with their work passionately, creatively, and collaboratively. In short, individuals are contributing what they were hired to do and more.

It sounds like a dream, right? This vision is contingent upon one important condition: Employees are physically and mentally able to contribute to their full potential.

To understand how this plays out, picture the following scenario: Zeal fades, and stress sneaks in as deadlines abound. Top performers become distracted, mistakes happen more frequently, and creativity no longer flows freely. Over time, individuals seem to miss more work due to sickness and are less eager to help their teammates. The very employees you invested in so heavily are performing at reduced capacity.

While it might sound dramatic, various studies that we'll explore in this chapter show that this scenario is pervasive in the workplace.

I share this not to alarm you, but rather to emphasize the importance of wellness at work and the potential for greatness if we create healthy environments for our employees. For any leader who wants to maximize employee performance and retain the most qualified and productive employees, encouraging wellness must be a business-critical objective.

So what's an employer to do? First, we have to define wellness in practical, approachable terms.

DEFINING WELLNESS AT WORK

Wellness at work refers to the policies, resources, and initiatives that help employees maintain physical and mental health. Employees who feel healthy and have work-life balance are more motivated, focused, and positive. As illustrated in the scenario above, they also can contribute in a more significant way. I am sure you know this from your own experience.

The companies that do this well are those that intentionally embed wellness in their day-to-day norms. According to the 2016 *Future of Wellness at Work* report by the Global Wellness Summit, traditional wellness programs receive inconsistent participation and results.[55] To correct for that, the same report advocates for a more holistic approach, integrated in the way the company operates. As you read this chapter, consider your values, employee preferences, and any unique factors that might contribute to employee wellness at your organization.

Speaking of a more holistic approach, your wellness efforts should support both the physical and the mental well-being of employees. While the two are intertwined, traditional programs tended to focus more on the physical element of wellness, perhaps because it seems easier to tackle. If we spend an average of ninety thousand hours at work in our lifetime, imagine the powerful sway one's work environment will have on our overall health!

We should keep up these efforts, no doubt. However, as leaders looking to improve the workplace, it's also important for us to include employee mental health in the conversation. Mental health is affected by both biological and environmental factors, and while employers can't affect the biological aspects, we do have significant control over the work environment. Employees come to work with a complex mix of personal experiences and challenges. If an organization doesn't have structures in place to assist with those challenges and help employees manage their well-being, it's going to affect their ability to function and decrease their performance. The rest of the chapter will explore common examples of how this plays out and what you as a leader can do to support your employees.

DEEP DIVE INTO STRESS

I'll start by examining stress. Not only is stress incredibly pervasive in the workplace—six in ten employees surveyed in a 2017 ComPsych study report high levels of stress[56]—but also it is the component of wellness that employers have the greatest ability to influence, both negatively and positively.

Fear of job loss adds stress for U.S. workers who still bear the scars of a historically bad recession in 2008 and experience significant job churn in the economy. I remember that on my college graduation day, my parents ceremoniously handed me our only family heirloom: a shiny gold watch. The watch originally had been given to my grandfather as recognition for his twenty-five years of employment with a large insurance company. My parents hoped that passing down this symbolic gift as I entered the workforce would inspire me to pursue my own twenty-five years of dedicated service at a big, stable company. It didn't work out that way for me—instead I founded and built several companies—but my parents' hope for me then speaks to our national economic anxiety now. Most workers today have given up the expectation of retiring and receiving a gold watch after decades with one company. That sense of job insecurity and uncertainty is another stressor.

From getting stuck in the morning commute to attending unavoidably long meetings, the pressure to deliver excellent work in a short time frame or on a small budget can drain even the most high-performing employees. Individuals who experience this feeling too often or too long can develop chronic stress levels that affect their health and their ability to deliver high-quality work.

A 2012 Yale study found that stress shrinks the brain in areas that control emotions, metabolism, and memory, resulting in emotional and physiological consequences.[57] The result is that stressed employees, similar to sleepy employees, simply don't have access to their full range of abilities.

Stressed employees aren't in a state to be engaged and communicative in their work. This limits their ability to create and maintain relationships with other employees, which is how trust and mutual support in the workplace are formed. Without trust, support, and communication, employees aren't capable of engaging in the random, inventive encounters companies such as Google and Pixar credit for their much-coveted creativity. The result is a community of employees who may be able to do their core job, but never rise to achieve their peak potential.

All of this translates to real consequences in financial results. Stressed workers incur twice the health care costs as unstressed workers, and stress-related sleepiness and distraction contribute to accidents on the job.[58] Tallied up, the American Institute of Stress estimates that workplace stress costs U.S. employers an estimated $200 to $300 billion per year in lowered productivity, increased absences and turnovers, and growing workers' compensation, insurance, and other stress-related expenses.[59]

Can employers and managers eliminate all sources of stress from every employee's job? Of course not, and it wouldn't be recommended. As psychologist Kelly McGonigal explains in her viral TED talk, a certain level of stress can give you extra energy and help you perform better.[60] We all know that certain responsibilities naturally demand more from some employees than others.

Regardless of the size of your organization, reclaiming even a portion of this loss by investing in lowering employees' stress levels would result in significant company-wide savings.

All the data surrounding stress in the workplace are enough to make anyone feel, well, stressed. But managers can do a lot to integrate wellness into the workplace and position your company as a source of confidence and comfort to employees. With that, let's shift into action mode by exploring the following ways to promote wellness at your company:

1. Provide resources.

2. Lead by example.

3. Encourage hobbies and interests outside of work.

PROVIDE RESOURCES

Your job as a leader and manager is not to become a health professional, but instead to provide easy access to resources and make employees aware of them.

When it comes to physical health, plenty of ideas are out there. My favorite examples include stocking the kitchen with healthy snack options instead of the usual vending machine fare, and encouraging employees to exercise through gamification, financial incentives, or subsidized gym memberships. Strategic Financial Services has a weekly "Wellness Wednesday" when it sponsors a wellness-oriented resource or activity.

On the mental health front, many health benefit packages have affordable options for employees to take advantage of. I encourage you to take it a step further and remove potential barriers by providing workplace counseling or referrals to help locate appropriate resources. Short-term therapy, long-term therapy, and psychoanalysis all reduce psychiatric symptoms of stress and improve work ability.[61] Furthermore, corporate counseling programs have been shown to reduce employee absenteeism significantly and to heighten employee mental health and self-esteem.[62]

Remember, in order for these resources to have an effect, employees need to know they exist. One company in our study, Romark Logistics in Westfield, New Jersey, provides a great example of educating employees about wellness and the resources the company offers. Every year Romark dedicates a full month to a specific wellness focus, such as mental health awareness. During this month, leaders highlight the mental health resources they provide, host educational seminars, and organize fundraisers around this topic.

"We invest significant resources when it comes to ensuring employees are provided the best benefits and wellness education that we can provide," relates President Marc Lebovitz.

I recommend providing outlets for your team members to voice their stress triggers, whether it's through an anonymous employee survey or a trusted colleague. This will help you provide targeted solutions and resources to address the challenges at hand. For example, if workload is your team's concern, offer workshops on task management, delegation, prioritization, and organizational skills. If work-life balance is your team's concern, work together to determine a reasonable balance and encourage each team member to commit to small, consistent, and achievable goals to get there.

Providing wellness benefits and resources is a great first step. However, often it's not a lack of resources that causes stress in the workplace; it's a lack of support to use them. After all, a flexible or unlimited vacation policy won't improve employee stress levels if employees feel that it's frowned upon to take paid time off from work. Change has to come from the top down, which is why it's so important that leaders at all levels in the organization understand the powerful benefits that come from enhancing employee wellness and initiate a conversation about it.

For starters, leaders and managers should explicitly outline expectations for taking breaks, limiting after-work hours, and other methods for lowering stress. The real impact, however, comes from how leadership embraces these principles day to day. If the entire company is on board with work-life balance, but you still have managers sending emails at 9 p.m. and expecting an immediate response, your efforts won't achieve results. These are the small signs that employees will look for before adopting healthy habits themselves.

Reinforcing these values is essential for wellness and productivity. Most employees can relate to a CEO giving a speech extolling work-life balance while knowing their own manager pings them 24/7. As a leader and manager, one of the smallest things you can do is to model the suggested behavior by taking breaks. Again, Romark Logistics provides a wonderful example in action. Every day includes a stretch program where employees across levels, including the president, and departments take a break to stretch together.

Most leaders still don't encourage employees to take regular breaks.[63] This is further evidence of how managers can be your best front-line resources for understanding employee stressors and troubleshooting solutions to increase productivity. They should be supported in respecting work-life balance. This may mean adjusting timelines, expectations, or client relationships to make room for life, or it may simply require some training to help managers build new habits that encourage a work-life balance. For example, showing managers how to have one-on-one conversations about how their employees are feeling physically and mentally can be just as important as a manager knowing how to get status updates on projects. To prevent burnout, TCG's vice president of Employee Happiness monitors employee time sheets to ensure that no one consistently works too many hours. If someone does, the VP partners with the employee's manager to reduce stressors and lighten the load.

Recognition also plays a large role in shaping employee behavior. It's easy to publicly recognize the person who pulled an all-nighter or worked the weekend to churn out a key deliverable, but if you're looking to avoid an always-on culture, this can reinforce the wrong message. Leaders should champion quality, not just effort.

ENCOURAGE EMPLOYEES TO HAVE HOBBIES AND INTERESTS

Encouraging your employees to have hobbies outside of work may sound like an awkward form of micromanagement, but employees who have other interests and who see work as a part of their identity, rather than their entire life, are better able to face stress and overcome challenges.

Although you can't force employees to have interests outside of work, you can create space within the workplace to encourage this behavior. Urge employees to develop a well-rounded life by including personal interests in their yearly objectives and inviting them to share their hobbies and interests with co-workers during work hours.

Like most transformative business achievements, wellness isn't a one-and-done task you can check off your to-do list. It is a process of seeing the enormous potential within your employees and troubleshooting the constantly changing challenges within your workplace that keep them from performing at consistently high levels.

By taking small but carefully planned steps toward your company's unique vision of wellness, you can be a powerful source of support to your employees, empowering them to achieve their performance potential and apply it to serve your company's mission.

FEATURE STORY
WELLNESS

TCG: Core Values Core to Employee Happiness

By Monelle Taylor, Marketing Communications Specialist

Our commitment to core values carries into how we reward each other. Fully armed with the knowledge of the company's core values and the practice of rewarding notable work, each employee is given a Bonus.ly account to award points to co-workers who exhibit the core values. Bonus.ly is a platform whereby staff can give micro-bonuses to their colleagues and publicly acknowledge them for exhibiting the company's core values. Thus the core values of the company are reinforced, shared, and integrated into the culture. At the annual All-Hands Meeting, point leaders in each category are acknowledged and given an additional gift for their extraordinary work. Bonus.ly points can be traded in for gift cards at major retailers, or the cash value can be donated to a charity. Some employees have accumulated enough points to trade in for an extra vacation day.

One of the unique aspects of TCG that has shaped our culture is that employees are completely dispersed at various client worksites, or they telecommute. TCG's model is that everyone works from home unless needs from a client require them to be on site (usually for security reasons or for the occasional meeting). This has significantly helped staff manage their work-life balance and meet the needs of their family while still being successful at work. For example, eliminating the commute to work, which in the District of Columbia metro area averages 62 minutes per day, frees up time for staff to start preparing dinner, go to their kids' game, or meet other personal responsibilities. Plus, it helps staff get to know their colleagues on a more intimate level. You might get to meet someone's dog or cat during a video chat or see how they've chosen to decorate their house.

Because staff are dispersed, TCGers may go a long time without physically seeing each other. For that reason, the company sponsors several social activities throughout the year so that staff get face time with each other. And since these are social activities, not professional meetings, staff tend to relax and let loose when they do get together. For example, the company started "TCG Sprees," an arrangement whereby any TCGer can host a social event and have the company pay for it, up to $1,000. TCG sponsors one TCG Spree a month and recently started TCG Charity Sprees for those employees who want to get together in favor of a good cause. Each spree gives us a chance to have new experiences, try new foods, or learn about other cultures.

Additionally, once per month the Employee Happiness Department hosts "Lunch with Dan," a gathering of up to ten TCGers from various parts of the company to meet for lunch with the president of the company. Staff get to meet colleagues that they would not normally interact with, and they are encouraged to ask questions of Dan about . . . well, anything!

The downside to staff working from home and having flexible schedules is that they tend to work more than they would if they were in the office. This sounds like a win for managers and productivity, but it does have deleterious effects. Staff can easily burn out and may start to resent the work or the company. To mitigate this problem, our vice president of Employee Happiness monitors time sheets for everyone in the company and flags employees who consistently work more than forty hours per week. She'll work with their manager to see what can be done to lighten their load and reduce potential stressors.

This focus on work-life balance has not gone unnoticed by employees or the community. The results of a recent anonymous employee survey conducted by a third party show that 100 percent of TCGers say, "I am able to take time off from work when I think it's necessary," and 99 percent of staff say that TCG "is a psychologically and emotionally healthy place to work."

We have an Employee Happiness Department. Not only that, it's led by an Executive Team member, which reflects the company's deliberate and strategic decision to make the well-being of employees, in and out of the workplace, a priority.

The Employee Happiness Department organizes social and team-building events, plans activities for staff and their families, administers TCG's many perks, facilitates the company's social intranet site, and participates in career reviews with staff and their respective managers. Their work has helped to foster a sense of community among staff who are dispersed geographically and across projects, and to demonstrate to the staff that the company appreciates their contributions.

Members of this team meet with each TCGer at least three times per year: during their annual career review, once on their birthday, and on their un-birthday. Birthday and un-birthday coffees are just a chance to check in to see how things are going and discuss any specific interests they might have professionally or personally. If they have any concerns, they can discuss them at that time. Since the Employee Happiness Department is represented in the Executive Team, the sentiments of employees are heard by those charged with the management of the company. In many ways, this department is both the keeper and a reflection of the company culture. Its members are the embodiment of TCG's core values.

The results of their work have helped land TCG on some of the top workplace lists, including Entrepreneur Magazine and CultureIQ's Top Company Cultures list, The Washington Post's Top Workplace list, and Fortune and Great Place to Work's best workplace for technology, medium and small businesses, and women lists. Additionally, TCG's voluntary turnover rate in 2017 was only 10.4 percent, which is below the national standard. Even if employees leave TCG, sometimes they come back! We've had several employees who left the company and later came back. One employee left for a promotion but ended up returning because here at TCG he felt appreciated, while at the other company he felt like a cog in a wheel.

CHAPTER 7: WELLNESS
TAKEAWAYS AND TIPS

- Ask your team or organization how you are performing respective to this dimension: A company that values wellness has the policies and resources to help people maintain physical and mental health. How would you rate your organization's wellness?

- Clearly express your expectations to both employees and managers that employees take breaks and relax periodically throughout the day.

- Start a "wellness channel," using internal communication tools such as Slack, where employees can organize grassroots fitness activities or initiate group stretch breaks.

- Ask leaders, HR managers, and other managers to lead by example and take breaks and walks, if possible, inviting other employees to join them for a short time.

- Provide healthy snacks and drinks in a centrally located break room, which will encourage employees to take breaks and interact with colleagues throughout the day.

- Sponsor personal technology such as Apple Watches or Fitbits and reward high step counts to encourage friendly, healthy competition among team members.

- Encourage managers to conduct walking meetings when appropriate or add a group walk to the first or last minutes of each meeting.

- Dedicate an empty office or break room to a relaxation space and outfit it with soft lighting, couches, and tables where employees can talk or rest periodically throughout the day.

- Use department-wide time off as a reward for the completion of large projects, large sales goals, or seasonally busy times.

- Incorporate daily breaks and vacation time into performance reviews so that all employees hear the importance of taking breaks and vacations in a one-on-one meeting with their managers.

- Consider letting employees leave early on a Friday at different times of the year. For a much bigger change, consider following in Amazon's footsteps and adopting a thirty-hour week policy during certain slow business seasons.[64]

- Incorporate wellness into your team bonding events. For example, consider hosting a "yoga hour" once a month.

- Offer referrals for therapy or counseling, and train managers and HR on directing employees to those resources.

- Create a weekly ritual of "Wellness Wednesday," or any day of the week, where the company sponsors or encourages a staff-wide wellness activity.

CHAPTER 8:

PERFORMANCE ORIENTATION

A FEW YEARS AGO I VISITED A COMPANY IN COLORADO AND PARTICIPATED IN ITS ALL-HANDS MEETING. At the conclusion of the meeting, the CEO invited up the monthly winner of the Mr. Potato Head Award. As you might guess, I was confused at the mention of a potato head. I became even more confused when the entire auditorium of employees stood, clapped, and cheered as someone took the stage to receive nothing other than a plastic potato head. The Mr. Potato Head Award, I quickly learned, is a peer-recognition program in which last month's winner awards this toy to a colleague who has gone above and beyond the call of duty.

Katherine Daniel, Director of Marketing at N2 Publishing in Wilmington, North Carolina, shares a similar, cool model for infusing performance into culture. "N2 Publishing's culture is something that exists within our team members," she explains. "It's positive, radiating, and motivating. It's a shared attitude, and it's something we deeply feel is worth celebrating and recognizing.

"We love to honor team members who exemplify our culture and work hard to reach their goals. Every month at our home office team meeting, a gathering of all three-hundred-plus team members who work out of our corporate office, we include a segment known as "Catching People Doing Things Right." This is when we recognize a team member who was noticed making N2 a better place to work because of his or her humility, willingness to help others, and ability to put a smile on someone's face.

"N2's most prestigious recognition, though, comes in the form of an old, battered metal lunch pail. You've likely seen the classic 1932 *Lunch Atop a Skyscraper* image: Eleven construction workers casually sit in a row along a crossbeam, eating meals brought from home in their metal lunch pails while suspended at a whopping eight hundred feet above bustling New York City streets. Though the identities of many of the men pictured are still uncertain, there's zero doubt that they were fearless, hard workers who truly went out on a limb to get their job done. That's the kind of dedication and commitment N2 is proud to recognize with our acclaimed Lunch Pail Award. Given every year to a few team members, as well as some of our franchise business owners, this award represents the old-school work ethic embodied by the men in that historic photo."

Performance awards and incentives are part of almost every organization's operations. From the perspective of culture, I'm more interested in how companies such as N2 are reshaping the ways they encourage employee performance. They're acknowledging the psychological factors of employee motivation and considering how the culture in the team and the company reinforces motivation and engagement through goals. Even so, CultureIQ's Top Company Cultures data show that out of our list of ten culture dimensions, performance orientation ratings at organizations score in the bottom three, meaning this is incredibly hard to get right.

In this chapter I will explore what it means to be a performance-oriented company. I'll provide best practices around goal setting, recognition, and development, and offer inspiration for how to apply them in your organization.

WHAT IS A PERFORMANCE-ORIENTED COMPANY?

Performance-oriented companies ensure that people know how to succeed in their roles and are motivated to give their best. In order for that to be the case, the following three conditions must be in place: First, there are clear goals and metrics across all levels. Second, people are recognized for their contributions. Third, employees are supported in their growth areas.

Let's be honest: When most of us as employees hear the subject shift to performance management and performance orientation, we start getting a knot in our stomach, thinking about our next review or how we're stacking up against our peers. That's where culture comes in. Performance orientation is not about sacrificing employee happiness for the benefit of the bottom line.

My definition paints a different picture, one in which a focus on engagement and a focus on performance go hand in hand. As we dive into the conditions presented above, the interaction between performance and engagement will become even more clear.

GOALS AND METRICS

It's well-known that goals and metrics are critical for a company's performance and organizational alignment, but they also play an important role in employee engagement. Clear goals reduce ambiguity and provide meaning to one's work, which contributes to increased motivation. They help employees understand what they are working toward; on a micro level, how everyday tasks contribute to their outlined goals; and on a macro level, how their output contributes to organizational performance.

Research by Gallup tells this story clearly. By asking more than eight thousand employees about their relationship with their manager, researchers found that "employees who work for a manager who helps them set performance goals are seventeen times more likely to be engaged than disengaged."[65] I'll repeat that for effect: seventeen times more likely to be engaged than disengaged!

Not only that, the same Gallup research demonstrates the importance of sticking to these goals. The report states that "when managers don't hold employees accountable for performance, about seven in ten employees (69 percent) are actively disengaged; only 3 percent are engaged."[66]

If that doesn't inspire you to train and encourage managers to set goals, track metrics, and have performance conversations, I don't know what will!

As mentioned earlier, goals serve two important purposes on the individual level: They create clarity and provide meaning. Employees should understand exactly what they are trying to achieve and why they are trying to achieve that specific outcome; otherwise your people will have no idea how to prioritize their time and resources. My tips for increasing clarity are simple: align on an individual's goals and metrics during onboarding, train managers in communicating goals, and create a central place where employees can reference their goals and objectives.

Goals, whether individual or group, also serve as a guiding star. When communicated well, they assign direction and meaning to otherwise menial tasks. Meaning is critical in driving employee performance.

My favorite illustration of the importance of meaning in work is Duke University professor Dan Ariely's experiment on motivation in the *Journal of Economic Behavior and Organization*.[67] You can hear him explain the research in his 2012 TED talk: *What Makes Us Feel Good About Our Work*.[68]

In this experiment, researchers paid participants to build Lego Bionicles® using a declining wage schedule ($2.00 for the first Bionicle, $1.89 for the second, and so forth) under two conditions. In the first condition, the completed Bionicles were accumulated and displayed on the participant's desk. In the second condition, the researcher deconstructed the Bionicle in front of the participant directly following completion.

The result: Participants in the first condition built significantly more Bionicles than those in the second. This teaches us that if we don't understand what a task, a presentation, or a project leads to, we won't be motivated to increase our output. Further, those with a pre-existing affinity for building Legos built more Bionicles in the first condition, and they didn't in the second condition. This means that even if people enjoy their work, they will not be motivated to perform if it feels pointless.

In order for goals to carry meaning and motivate employees, employees must understand what their work contributes to on a grander level, the big picture. The best way to do this is to make explicit links among an individual's output, the team's goals, and the organization's strategy.

Another invaluable piece of the motivation puzzle is how employees are recognized for their achievements.

REWARDS AND RECOGNITION

In 2014, BCG surveyed more than two hundred thousand employees across the world as part of its Global Mobility and Employment Preferences survey.[69] These data found appreciation for one's work to be the single most important factor for employee happiness on the job. In comparison, job security ranked seventh out of twenty-six factors, and attractive fixed salary came in eighth.

This finding wouldn't surprise anyone familiar with Maslow's Hierarchy of Needs (See chart below).[70] Recognition helps to satisfy both "Needs for love, affection, and belongingness" and "Esteem needs." We want to feel valued in a group, and recognition is a clear signal that we are valued.

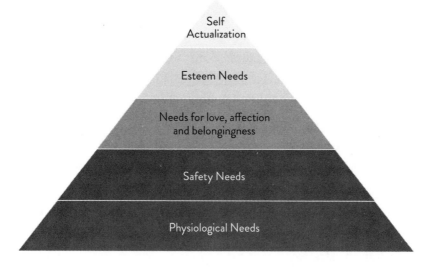

Our need for recognition and its impact on our happiness at work presents a huge opportunity for organizations. Bersin by Deloitte research shows that companies in the top quintile for building a "recognition-rich culture" experience 31 percent lower voluntary employee turnover rates.[71]

What's the secret to creating a recognition-rich culture so that employees feel appreciated, motivated to give their best, and inspired to stick around? Extensive research focuses on how to best deploy recognition programs to motivate team members, and one thing stands out: as with most people-related topics, there is no one-size-fits-all approach.

For one, your recognition structure will depend on your goal and team structure. Even after you decide what you want to recognize people for, you have to determine how. There are many different types of rewards, each serving a different purpose depending on the context. Some of the most common categories are intangible rewards, such as public acknowledgement and increased flexibility; cash rewards or bonuses; and non-cash rewards, such as tickets to a concert.

Instead of going through every combination and the pros and cons of each, I'll focus on four important considerations when designing your reward and recognition program:

1. ACKNOWLEDGE THAT EMPLOYEE MOTIVATION AND RECOGNITION PREFERENCES VARY.

Let's postulate two employees in the same level and role at your company. We'll call them Claudia and Dinesh. While Claudia and Dinesh might be accountable for the same metrics, I would bet that what intrinsically motivates Claudia to do her job (rewards aside) differs—whether slightly or significantly—from what motivates Dinesh to do his job. Further, the way each prefers to be recognized for a job well done probably differs as well. For example, Claudia might like acknowledgement from her manager during their one-on-one meeting, while Dinesh would welcome a public shout-out at the all-hands company meeting.

Employee motivation and recognition preferences can change throughout the employee life cycle. In CultureIQ's 2017 Top

Company Cultures study, we found that employees' perception of their company's performance orientation drops most significantly after one year's tenure compared with the other nine culture dimensions.[72]

This could be for a variety of reasons, including that as employees' tenure increases in the organization, it becomes harder to feel motivated or recognized for their contributions.

To account for these variations, your recognition program should allow some flexibility in the types of rewards employees receive for a job well done. Formal rewards aside, it is essential for managers to understand their direct reports' preferences about what motivates them and how they like to be recognized.

2. MESSAGE IT WITH CLARITY, MEANING, AND APPRECIATION.

When it comes to rewards and recognition, the how is just as important as the what. When recognizing someone for doing something, you essentially are saying, "Keep doing that!" or "Do that again!" In other words, recognition signals what the company prioritizes and encourages in a certain set of behaviors. When you message a reward, you should be clear exactly what is being rewarded. Be as specific as possible so the recipient and others understand what behaviors to replicate and what goals to achieve.

In addition to being specific, you want to be real. Use clear, direct language and avoid buzzwords and jargon. Harvard professor Ashley Whillans recommends that regardless of the form of the reward, it should be communicated in a way that reinforces the appreciation it signifies. Otherwise you run the risk of the reward feeling transactional.[73]

3. CONSIDER THE IMPLICIT SIGNALS YOUR RECOGNITION PROGRAM SENDS.

Speaking of messaging, the implicit message of rewards is just as important as the explicit message. Consider individual incentives versus group incentives. Individual incentives highlight an individual's contribution and encourage competition. While group incentives highlight the collective contribution and encourage collaboration, they might discourage someone's motivation to go above and beyond because individual achievements can get lost in the mix. Each option sends a unique message and serves a different purpose. You'll want to think about what makes the most sense given your context, and often, a combination of these options works best.

Tech company CIO Solutions in Central California provides a useful example. The leadership balanced individual and team rewards during a tight deadline. Individuals achieved a sense of progress by earning an army figurine when they accomplished their goals, and the entire team earned a celebration when all of the army figurines were spoken for. CIO Solutions incentivized all employees to do their best because they could earn multiple figurines. The company also incentivized them to help others complete their goals so the group could celebrate together. This is a wonderful example of how the goals and recognition align with the type of work the company hopes to see.

"Once all the army men were gone, around twelve weeks later, we gave a large company-wide prize," writes CEO Eric Egolf. "The prize was a company 'booze cruise' celebration. The theme was a success, and not just because we didn't lose any clients. It turns out that the theme itself implicitly said so much about our company culture, and it reinforced on a weekly basis our values to all the employees, new and old alike."

4. HARNESS SOCIAL POWER TO INSPIRE AND MOTIVATE OTHERS.

Recognition programs affect not only those rewarded, but also everyone who hears about them. Each time someone's accomplishments are acknowledged, it can be a learning opportunity for others. You can use this in your favor to create a recognition-rich culture, in which employees feel inspired by hearing others being recognized.

To harness this network effect, consider ways to make recognition moments more visible and shareable. For example, Harvard professor Ashley Whillans explains that one of the benefits of non-cash rewards when compared with cash rewards is that people feel more comfortable discussing them with their peers.[74] Similarly, visible rewards, such as N2's lunch pail, are great because they don't even require the recipient to discuss them to be noticed.

It's important to note that the program must be perceived as fair; otherwise, the social power of recognition can have a backfire effect.

GROWTH AND DEVELOPMENT

The final piece of the performance puzzle is employee growth and development. This plays out in a few ways.

For one, investing in your employees' development gives them the opportunity to acquire a wider skill set. With more skills, they are better equipped for dealing with problems and are thus more productive. Furthermore, well-trained workers can extend their roles by covering more areas, which leads to even more productivity.

On the other hand, employees who feel unfit and unmotivated will procrastinate and become apathetic, and this is likely to result in low productivity. By investing in appropriate training for your employees, you decrease the need for constant supervision.

Let's put an end to the false notion that trained employees tend to look for better job opportunities. The truth of the matter is that when a company invests in its employees, the employees feel more empowered and appreciated, which increases their loyalty to their current employer. If a current employer provides opportunities to progress professionally, then employees have less incentive to look elsewhere. It comes down to how human beings behave and think: We want to feel that we matter and that we belong.

In fact, the Gallup report *How Millennials Want to Work and Live* found that "opportunities to learn and grow" is one of the top three reasons millennial employees choose to stay at a company.[75] Remember, hiring a new employee is more expensive than maintaining an existing one, even if it means investing in the existing employee's development.

The Gallup research found that we have a lot of work to do in this arena. Only four in ten millennials surveyed agreed that they had learned something new in the past thirty days, and fewer than half strongly agreed that they had opportunities to learn and grow in the past year.

How do you address this? I propose three key ways: feedback, regular manager conversations, and training and resources.

Before I dive into these themes, it's worth noting that they are mentioned in other chapters in slightly different contexts. Like many of the topics I cover in this book, these initiatives don't fall squarely into one culture dimension; rather, they benefit the organization in many ways. I encourage you to read on with that lens.

1. SPECIFIC FEEDBACK

Feedback is the critical lever to employee growth and development. Specific feedback helps employees understand exactly what they should start, stop, and continue doing to accomplish their goals.

The key is to normalize giving and receiving feedback in your organization, so that it becomes an expected part of conversations. In this scenario, employees have access to information that will help them improve and develop on a regular basis. One of the best things you can do to support a culture of development is train people, especially managers, on how to give and receive feedback.

This leads to my next point.

2. REGULAR MANAGER CONVERSATIONS

In many ways, managers are the keepers of their direct reports' development. For that reason, they should have regular conversations with members of their team to understand their motivations, provide them feedback, and coach them in their growth goals.

And guess what? The benefits of manager conversations extend beyond the participating individuals. Gallup found that employees who have regular meetings with their manager perform better for their team and the company.[76]

When it comes to manager-employee relationships, this is just the tip of the iceberg. We will dive deeper into this topic in Chapter 10: Support.

3. LEARNING AND DEVELOPMENT PROGRAMMING

Feedback and manager conversations are the foundation for an employee's development, but what happens when the growth areas require support beyond a manager's means? That is where a more comprehensive learning and development program comes into play.

Consider the following elements when creating your learning and development program: training in hard and soft skills, online content, mentorship options, a discretionary learning fund, and industry resources and networks.

I've seen some great examples of development programs that have zero costs. One idea is creating a process for employees to sign up for short-term projects or assignments that align with their development goals. Another, my personal favorite example, is reverse mentoring. In a reverse mentoring program, a junior employee with an area of expertise mentors someone in a more senior role. My marketing manager is decades younger in her career than I, yet she is much more fluent in the world of social media, and she coaches me on navigating this critical component of our business. These programs not only provide valuable learning to the recipients, but also give mentors great satisfaction from teaching.

Digital marketer Direct Agents, based in New York City, sprouted a continuous learning and training initiative out of a fertile "culture of excellence that is driven by our senior leaders and supported by our core values and mission," writes Sara Martinez-Noriega, their director of human resources.

"Values like collaboration, innovation, and passion, along with a mission to be independent, entrepreneurial, and diverse, have helped land Direct Agents among those selected in the coveted Crain's 2018 Best Places to Work list."

Direct Agents viewed employees' well-being as a top-tier priority and acted accordingly with changes in the health value of company snacks, expanded support for remote working and work-life innovations, and better health insurance.

"On a deeper level, we looked to invest in not only day-to-day tactical trainings, but in the fostering of strategic thinking through reviewing and discussing Harvard Business School case studies in small group sessions. One of these case studies was on Google's Project Oxygen, which looked to uncover which traits make a good manager. From our discussions around this case study, we were able to implement our own iteration of Project Oxygen and give our managers guides and resources for how to improve their management skills based on the reviews they received from their direct reports.

"Our last engagement survey reported Direct Agents at 82 percent employee engagement, 13 percentage points above our benchmark comparisons to other media and creative companies in 2018. More importantly, it highlighted areas for improvement, and we were able to create several initiatives like those around learning and development: creating clear growth paths for each role within the company, feedback and recognition, and celebrating wins of all sizes and impacts."

FEATURE STORY
PERFORMANCE ORIENTATION

VIBCO: The Crying Customer

By Karl Wadensten, CEO

VIBCO manufactures industrial and construction vibrators with about eighteen hundred finished items in our product line, over forty-six patents, and three-hundred-sixty thousand customers globally. We are in the MRO business: maintenance, repair, and operation. In our business, when somebody calls, they need it now. They don't need excuses; they don't need delays; they don't need anything else. They need product because we're holding up an operation, a process, people, and money. We're holding up a lot of things that matter in the contracting world.

Back in 2000 we didn't have clarity of what our true north was. We didn't have a deep understanding that when customers needed things, they needed them now. They didn't need complexity and confusion. They didn't need to concern themselves with that. All they needed to know was that we put the vibrator in the box and got the boxes out to them in the right quantity, at the right time, at the right price. I'm using these words explicitly because these are the things that customers want to know. Now that I've laid out a little background of our business, you can see where VIBCO was nearly twenty years ago. This is the story of how we obtained a deeper understanding into what our business culture really was and what our business wasn't.

My employee Giovanni, working in our sales department, had been speaking to a customer throughout the entire week and even the week prior, and the conversation reached a fever pitch on Friday as it was the last work day of the week. With each call, the customer placed that Friday, you could tell by his voice he was getting more and more panicked. He sensed from the answers Giovanni was giving him that the order was not going to ship even though we had been telling him, "We're trying to ship this out." We were trying, but we'd missed numerous promises before.

As Giovanni tells it, "Once I realized that it was not going to happen, I had to, in good conscience, tell him the truth. The final bell was ringing, employees were clocking out, and we didn't have any more time. I wanted to tell the customer that, hey, we tried, but there's nothing else we could do to get it out today. That's when he began to get very upset—not in anger but with sadness—and he literally broke down and cried. I started crying too as he explained to me that he had a good friend that was an engineer on the job that had recommended him for the project."

"It was tough to hang up the phone. I felt like it was a 911 call, and I should just be there for him," explained Giovanni. "He finally realized that it wasn't going to happen and said goodbye."

Giovanni had plans to go out to a quarterly lunch with the shipping group of six other workers. On the way to lunch, the crew was talking about the job, and Giovanni said, "You know, we should call Chief (their nickname for me)." I was home sick with bronchitis, but I called Giovanni back.

Giovanni explained that the customer's relatively small vibrator order was going to hold up a billion-dollar bridge project. He was sad. Giovanni said that in all his time here a customer had never cried over the phone to him. Karl told the shipping group to finish their meals, meet him back at the factory, and call whoever they can to get back to the VIBCO factory in Rhode Island to try and deliver the job.

We had one person deburring, and I did welding. Giovanni fetched pieces and parts for them because there were brackets and other accessories that needed to be fabricated and packaged to go along with the vibrator units. Our culture journey began that day with Giovanni having empathy and concern for a customer, and being clear and honest with the customer. Giovanni was stuck in a process that wasn't delivering the results that our customers expected and needed. That was Giovanni's defining moment.

Giovanni called the customer back and said, "The president of the company knows now. We're going to get this product to you." That's a key thing. Giovanni reached out.

The defining moment for me was that Giovanni put his honesty and integrity, on the line for this customer, assuring him that something was going to get done. I couldn't just leave it like that – I couldn't let Giovanni down like that – I couldn't let the customer down like that. It becomes a ripple effect of people who are disappointed and frustrated. I had to break the cycle, and now my word was on it.

The loyal VIBCO employees who came back that Friday started working at lightning speed on this order. The welder didn't come back, but I had been trained in welding. Even with severe bronchitis, I put on a welding hood and respirator and started welding. Giovanni, Clark, and the others assembled these pieces and did all the things that we needed to do.

All the while, we worked with the knowledge of one critically important detail. The UPS plane leaves at 7:00 p.m. on Friday. We had to get UPS to help us out. We were 30 minutes away from the airport, and we started midday working on this order, putting in the final touches to get this order ready to go on time.

The loyal VIBCO crew had the last box buttoned up 6:32 p.m. I am thinking (we all were) So a 30-minute ride to the airport, the plane leaves at 7, do the math: 7:02, barring no traffic on a Friday night in New England. Thank God you know a guy in Rhode Island, the smallest state in the union! We knew the guy, Billy, that was the head of logistics and sales for UPS, and on our drive up there, I was dialing his number frantically, saying that I was on my way. "You've got to hold the plane. You've got to hold the plane because now my word, Giovanni's word, and the hope of all our people here at VIBCO is that this is happening tonight."

We couldn't let the customer go into the weekend not knowing what was happening. We couldn't call back again saying we missed the plane. That wasn't going to happen. The sense of urgency wasn't one person's urgency; it was a village of urgency.

I had to quickly review with UPS that this was happening. I said, "Billy, do whatever you got to do." Whatever Billy did that night, that plane was held, and we made it there at 7:03 p.m. They were checking in boxes as they were loading them onto the cargo bay of the plane.

I drove back to the shop right after the delivery to the small crew of warriors who made this happen – who understood the urgency, understood the integrity, understood that we all had our names to this, that this was going to happen. I would have figured that we'd be celebrating like we just won the Super Bowl. I walked into the factory and only saw long faces. We knew that this wasn't a winning strategy to gain customers and retain customers. We knew that we had let this guy down three times before. It wasn't individual people that had let him down. It was our process.

I went back home to bed for the weekend. I took my medicine and stayed in bed with bronchitis, and the entire time I was lying there, I was thinking about what had just happened.

As I drove to work the following Monday, I questioned whether I was a good leader. How could this happen? We saw everything on the surface. It seemed that we were doing a good job, and everybody's working hard, but the feedback and reflection from customers wasn't showing us that. I didn't know if I wanted to be the leader of an organization like this.

Even though what we just did was Herculean, we weren't laying the track work for long-term sustained growth and holding up to our promises to customers. Did I want to run an organization where we didn't uphold the responsibility and promises to the customers every time, at all costs, no matter what? And if I didn't want to be in that organization, why should my people want to be in that organization? If we can't work together as a team and share and learn together, then it's not meant for me to lead this organization.

I was thinking of all the reasons that I didn't have the stamina or energy to lead an organization that would do this again and again and again, unintentionally. Whatever success we attained would be marginal at best because long-term sustained growth doesn't happen often without reflection or introspection of ourselves.

Then it hit me. What we had to do to survive was a process called *Same Day, Next Day*. It had to happen today in VIBCO, tomorrow in the truck, the next day at the customer. We did not previously have the clarity to see how time sensitive and urgent our customers were when they called for help and needed suggestions. They needed it now, not tomorrow, not next week, not next hour.

We're pain relief for customers, I thought. As I drove in, I could see it clear as day. When I arrived at VIBCO that Monday morning, I circled all the employees. We met in the cafeteria and discussed what had happened that Friday while everybody was home for the weekend, having fun, thinking that we were a hard-working organization, and feeling proud about the things we did right. We discussed and shared with them what happened with our customer. I shared the heartfelt, heartbreaking story about how we let our customer down. I shared the camaraderie and the get-to-it spirit that we had all given to make this happen and talked about our process. Everybody looked at me with blank faces. They didn't understand.

I wrote "same day, next day" on the board. I could see it wasn't resonating so I drew the picture on the board. I added the smiley faces with the Help! exclamation, and then I showed the happy face. I drew a picture of our factory (same day), a picture of the truck (tomorrow), and a picture of the customer's factory (next day). Then the light bulbs started going on, and finally we, as an organization, began to see our mission.

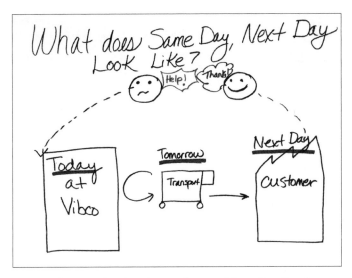

The original Karl Wadensten drawing of Same Day, Next Day

The sum of the pieces is greater than the whole. Everybody figured out what their pieces were. Some people had to do it the same minute, next minute. Some people had to do it the same hour, next hour, and we started clicking. Even small steps over the course of the year would snowball into major changes. We had a lot of confusion. We got a lot of ambiguity. We actually had finger-pointing, too. There were people that wanted to finger-point, and the finger-pointing was not going to get us out of this predicament that we were in, nor help with sustained growth.

VIBCO started with training based on the lessons in the book *Fish!* about Seattle's Pike Place Fish Market and the birth of the *Fish!* customer experience philosophy. I gave everybody the *Fish!* book that Christmas. All kinds of other nice things went out, but everybody was kind of surprised that first year that they got a gift-wrapped book. This *Fish!* philosophy was the beginning of a framework and a platform for us to think about. We didn't just read the book, we lived it and we still live it today. This wasn't something we were going to do for just one year; this became core to our values and our beliefs.

CHAPTER 8: PERFORMANCE ORIENTATION
TAKEAWAYS AND TIPS

- Ask your team or organization how you are performing respective to this dimension: In a performance-focused company, people know what determines success in their roles, and they are rewarded or recognized for achievements. How would you rate your organization's performance focus?

- Conduct an audit of the clarity of your company goals:
  - Do employees know their current goals? Do they know their team's goals? Do they know the company's goals?
  - Do they know why these are the goals?
  - Is there a place where employees can read these goals?
  - Do individuals know how they are performing in relation to their goals?
  - Do employees understand how the company is performing in relation to its goals?
  - Do managers know how to create goals?

- Ask managers to have conversations about what inspires their direct reports and brainstorm creative ways to meet that need.

- Create a peer recognition system. Start small: It can be as simple as passing around a plastic potato head.

- Provide employees the opportunity to sign up for short-term projects that support their growth goals.

- Train employees of all levels on giving and receiving feedback.

- Provide a discretionary learning fund that employees can use for training, conferences, networking, books, or any resources of their choosing.

CHAPTER 9:

COLLABORATION

*C*FOR THE PAST FEW YEARS, MY DATA TEAM AND I HAD BEEN ANALYZING THE TRENDS SHAPING THE FUTURE OF WORK— IT'S A TOPIC THAT MANY CONSULTANTS ISSUE PRONOUNCE-MENTS ABOUT THESE DAYS! It's also a dimension of culture that is particularly interesting to me for this book and everything that I do.

Our research produced two remarkable facts that highlight the complexity of the workforce today: First, 60 percent of employees need to coordinate with ten or more colleagues each day to complete their work. Second, 50 percent of employees need to coordinate their work with colleagues in other locations.[77]

Research from the London Business School found that these exact dimensions of a team—in addition to the diversity and expertise of individuals on the team—also make collaboration more challenging.[78] It makes sense on a purely logistical level, let alone an interpersonal level. The lesson is not to reduce the diversity or expertise in a given team, but instead to create processes, establish expectations, and encourage behaviors that help individuals collaborate within and between teams.

Collaboration is a measure of effective teamwork. It occurs when people and teams cooperate, share information, and work well together. At a collaborative company, employees feel safe to speak up among their colleagues and excited to contribute their experience or expertise.

Collaboration is a tricky dimension to unpack because it can feel like an outcome of everything else in your culture going well, rather than a factor you can influence independently. While other culture dimensions—especially work environment, communication, and responsibility—are woven within the quest for collaboration, there are clear levers you can pull to increase collaboration in your company.

I have done my homework on how to optimize team dynamics. I was fascinated with a number of studies. You might be familiar with Harvard professor J. Richard Hackman's "enabling conditions" model as one example.[79] Another is Google's Project Aristotle analysis about what makes a successful Google team.[80] A few major insights grew out of the reading for me. Based on these insights, I've organized the chapter according to the following "collaboration levers":

1. Psychological safety.

2. Shared purpose.

3. Clear roles.

4. Collaborative behavioral norms.

An organization's success hinges on the cross-pollination of ideas and teamwork to solve today's business challenge. As you read through the sections that follow, I challenge you to consider how these factors apply not only to people working well together within teams, but also between teams.

PSYCHOLOGICAL SAFETY

At Google, in an experiment code-named Project Aristotle, a cross-functional group of Googlers studied what makes some teams more effective than others. After interviewing one hundred eighty teams and analyzing myriad data, the researchers found psychological safety to be the most important ingredient of effective teams—so important that all other contributing factors hinge on this ingredient's presence.[81] This tells us that if you are not sure where to start in your collaboration journey, creating a baseline of psychological safety in your organization is the logical first step.

Psychological safety, a term coined in 1999 by professor Amy Edmondson of Harvard Business School, refers to individuals' willingness to be vulnerable and take risks in front of others on their team.[82] Imagine how a team's ability to problem-solve and partner increases when individuals feel safe asking questions, admitting mistakes, and taking risks.

From a business perspective, fostering psychological safety is why you do team-building events. These activities provide an opportunity for teammates not only to get to know each other better, but also to practice trust and risk-taking together in a low-stakes context, for example, during a soccer game rather than a client meeting. A wonderful example of how to scale team-building events at your company is DMC's activity fund.

As CEO Frank Riordan notes, "DMC is a custom engineering and software development company based in Chicago and with offices around the country. We've been in business since 1996, have about one hundred seventy people, and have received consistent recognition for our company culture.

"We implemented this system years back, when I had just started a family, and my availability to organize social events was diminished.

(And never mind my life interests; maybe we're getting to be a bit different than the young workforce we hire.) Our activity fund has some basic rules:

1. The activity must be legal.

2. The activity must include a minimum number of people from the office (varies depending on the size of office) and +1s are allowed to go.

3. The activity must be inclusive—every employee must be invited.

4. Pictures and/or videos must be taken, which can then be used in DMC promotional materials and website.

"While the activity fund started to lessen my required involvement, it has developed into something that has far exceeded my initial expectations. I originally envisioned people would continue with the types of events that I had been involved with: happy hours, movie nights, and bowling. And while those certainly do happen, because everyone is given the autonomy to decide what they would like to do, the breadth of events has been exciting to see. People have indoor rock-climbed, participated in ax-throwing competitions, played bubble soccer, and so much more."

DMC has a monthly "use it or lose it" budget that anyone in the office can use to organize events for employees to connect outside of work. What I love about this idea is that it doubles down on collaboration: The planning of the event requires people to come together and make something happen, and then the enjoyment of it fosters psychological safety.

A SHARED PURPOSE

In his research on team effectiveness, Richard Hackman identified five conditions that enable team effectiveness. One of these is a "a compelling direction, a purpose that is clear, challenging, and consequential—and that focuses on the ends to be achieved rather than the means the team must use in pursuing them."[83]

While Hackman's research centers around a "true team," rather than an entire company, I believe that a shared purpose is essential to enabling collaboration on a broader level. Remember our discussion of mission and value alignment earlier in the book: your mission should serve as a uniting purpose.

Sacha Zackariya, co-founder and CEO of currency retailer The Change Group, shares how the firm built a cohesive culture across a workforce of six hundred team members from an astonishing eighty countries through a vision, mission, values, and aspirations document. It includes a vision of "serving the international traveler worldwide" and a mission to "provide engaging and convenient financial services to international travelers and businesses."

"In the U.S. you hear about racism, and often it is related to skin color," Zackariya says. "But when you employ eighty nationalities, you quickly realize there are all kinds of racism. I remember running our Estonian company and living there for two years in 2002. The collapse of the USSR had resulted in a large number of the former invaders choosing to stay behind in Estonia and not return.

"In their search for a new identity, I regularly witnessed Russians being discriminated against in shops, in educational opportunities, and in employment. I made an active point of drawing a line in the sand and welcoming ethnic Russians and ethnic Estonians to work together in our company, with all being given the same opportunities to progress, no matter the past.

"Just across the water about the same time, we had decided to introduce a bonus scheme for staff in Finland. When the local manager found out about our plans, he strongly disagreed, saying, 'We are Finnish. Of course, we will all work hard. We don't need bonuses!' Nevertheless we chose to do so, against various advice, and against what our competitors were doing. Sales increased almost straight away, and we learned quickly that not everything you hear about cultural differences is true!"

To see how this plays out in another context, imagine that two project teams in the customer service department are tasked with optimizing different parts of the client life cycle. The department has a limited budget and a notoriously arduous approval process.

In Scenario A, the teams deliver two different and slightly redundant solutions, plus a lot of departmental friction. In Scenario B, they deliver a cohesive solution that addresses both challenges, spending less money and time along the way. The difference? The teams in Scenario B—even though they were tasked with different problems—operated through the lens of a shared purpose and identity. Their common purpose of improving the client experience enabled their goals to feel compatible with each other. In Scenario A, on the other hand, the two teams approached it as a competition, turning it into a less effective "race to the resources."

For CEO Catriona Harris at Uproar PR, her firm thrives on this lesson of internal collaboration rather than an exhausting battle for resources. According to Harris, "Uproar's culture of collaboration addresses a hurdle that agencies in the industry often face: the tendency of team members to be competitive to the point of being siloed off from their co-workers. Instead, Uproar encourages employees to lean on each other for expertise, new contacts, and other resources, and emphasizes the results that come from inter-team collaboration. At Uproar, employees never feel as if they are taking on the world alone. There is always someone who has been there before and is willing to give advice, someone with a contact you need, or someone willing to take on a task when it feels like there are no more hours left in the day."

In all this talk about purpose, you might be asking: What happens when employees are so focused on their individual goals that they view collaborating with others as a distraction? Carlos Valdes-Dapena of Corporate Collaboration Resources and his team set out to understand this common challenge through research.[84] Their findings highlight the need to recognize what motivates individuals and frame the need to collaborate accordingly. Furthermore, if individual goals are set up effectively, they should align naturally with the larger shared purpose. Your job as a leader is to remind people of your shared purpose and make the link to their project, team, and individual goals.

CLEAR ROLES

It's safe to say that taking ownership over your own and your team's work is a universally desired practice. However, in the absence of the proper organizational systems, ownership's less-desirable cousin, territorialism, might sneak in. This happens when people or groups feel a threat to their sense of security, a common occurrence during times of change and growth.

The best way to avoid territorial behaviors or "turf wars" is to establish clarity around one's role and the roles of those around the individual. These guidelines actually grant employees more freedom to collaborate. This plays out in a few ways. For one, without understanding of who owns what, individuals might be reluctant to step in for fear of stepping on metaphorical toes. Role clarity frees employees from internal politics and the need to protect their turf.[85] Additionally, when there is consensus around responsibilities, people know who to go to for help and resources.

If you don't believe me, read the feature culture story later in this chapter written by Russ Reeder. From his experience leading companies and integrating smaller divisions into larger organizations, he's learned the importance of providing clear expectations, roles, and communication channels, so that employees are set up for success.

COLLABORATIVE BEHAVIORAL NORMS

All of the factors above can be in place, but if people don't know how to collaborate, you won't get very far. That's where collaborative behavioral norms come into play. What are these collaborative behaviors?

Lynda Gratton from the London Business School gives us a good place to start. Her team studied fifty-five complex and highly collaborative teams and identified eight practices that contribute to their success. One such practice is equipping employees with the following skills necessary for collaboration: appreciating others, engaging in purposeful conversations, productively and creatively resolving conflicts, and managing workflow.[86]

Ensuring that employees have those skills is a great place to start, but I challenge you to get even more specific in understanding what works within the dynamics of your organization. To do this, identify the employees within your organization that others consider highly collaborative and determine what behaviors they have in common. Partner with your human resources team to support all employees in developing these skills.

If collaboration is really important to you, consider screening for these behaviors while interviewing candidates to join your organization, incorporating them into your values, and factoring them into teams' definitions of success.

Furthermore, as with all of these dimensions of culture, it's a leader's responsibility to model what effective collaboration looks like. One highly visible venue for this is company meetings. I once wrote an article for *Entrepreneur Magazine* explaining how meetings serve as a microcosm of your company's culture.[87]

Given how often they occur, how many stakeholders they involve, and how many decisions they determine, meetings are a powerful opportunity to model positive behaviors and drive culture change. Stride Consulting of New York City broke down the meeting process into granular parts when developing its weekly leadership scrum meeting. The format took more than a year to optimize and incorporated some of the skills listed earlier in this section. As a result, meetings at Stride Consulting are a hotbed of collaboration and productivity. The detail and testing that Stride invested in its meetings process is so in-depth, useful, and immediately applicable that I am including Stride as an additional feature story in this chapter.

Finally, remember that as a leader and manager, you also have an opportunity to shine the spotlight on collaborative efforts that you have observed. For example, in your next all-hands company meeting, highlight an interesting project that came about from cross-functional efforts. When celebrating any company success, mention the diversity of experience that was pulled in. This messaging signals that collaboration is important to the company's success, fueling a collective spirit of collaboration within the organization.

FEATURE STORY
COLLABORATION

Stride Consulting: Structure to Collaborate

By Debbie Madden, Founder and CEO

Bad meetings suck and are a huge waste of time, to the tune of thirty-one hours per month. On the other hand, good meetings are the true pulse of scale.

The most important meeting is the weekly leadership team scrum. The goal of this meeting is to vigorously debate the top-priority issues facing the business and quickly decide action items.

The goal is not to solve every issue. The goal is to align on defining the issue and then align on next steps. Sometimes issues get resolved, but often they are handed off to one person to move forward.

This weekly meeting is our secret sauce. It is how we get stuff done. It is how we scale. And here's a peek under the hood at how we get it done.

It's one thing to have a weekly meeting. It's an entirely other thing for that meeting to be truly efficient to enable real scale.

For us, it took a solid year to get this meeting to be great. Now that it's great, we spend almost zero time emailing back and forth, and we have almost no unproductive meetings.

The meeting is scripted. It's got an agenda, and the agenda is the same every week:

1. At minute zero, each person gets one minute to share personal good news.

2. At minute five, we review KPI insights. We keep a Key Performance Indicator dashboard and review trends and draw insights.

3. At minute ten, we discuss roadblocks. A roadblock is something causing you to be stuck. Tell the team what it is, and the team's job is to help you get unstuck. If we can't unstick it quickly, the issue gets added to our issues list.

4. At minute twenty, we do a quick review of what we got done last week.

5. At minute twenty-five, we go over our open action items.

6. At minute thirty, we build and prioritize our issues list. These are the top-priority topics facing the business, both strategically and tactically. We prioritize issues that are tied to our annual initiatives. We also prioritize issues that absolutely must get resolved within the next five business days.

7. From minute thirty-five to eighty-five, so for a full fifty minutes, we debate each issue one at a time, in priority order. The person who raised the issue gets thirty seconds to share what's on his/her mind. The goal is to debate the issue and align as quickly as possible to the point where we can assign an action item or resolve the issue. Debate must be vigorous yet productive. Now's not

the time to be shy. Say what's on your mind, ask questions, and be productive and constructive.

8. Each action item coming out of debate has one owner and a due date.

TIME EACH DEBATE

We actually set a timer. An alarm goes off after five minutes, and we majority vote to keep discussing or move on. We want to allow enough time to get into the weeds, but not so much time that we are "selling past the close."

RATE EACH MEETING

At the end of each meeting, we rate ourselves, from one to five. We do it rock, paper, scissors-style and call it "Fist of Fives." We each raise one hand and put up from one to five fingers to show how valuable we felt the meeting was. Anyone who votes less than a five gets thirty seconds to say what it would take personally to get to a five.

The better this meeting becomes, the faster we pulse, the faster we make decisions, the more we get done, the faster we scale.

For me, the key lesson learned here is: Have the courage to stick with it, and forgive inefficiencies. This meeting is easy to get off the ground, yet hard to get right. For us, it took a solid year to get this meeting to great. How long will it take you?

FEATURE STORY
CULTURE COLLABORATION

Making It Work With GoDaddy

By Russ Reeder, former President and COO of Media Temple

I am a big believer that a strong, diverse team can accomplish great things, but only if the team members trust each other, communicate well, and have a great work ethic that allows people to fully engage and enjoy work. In other words, only if the team has a strong culture. Throughout my experience in business, I have gathered many stories related to culture. The most compelling— and hopefully helpful—have to do with sustaining a culture in challenging circumstances. Specifically in this case, operating as a subsidiary of a larger company.

When I was president of Media Temple, everyone in the company knew what we did, what we valued, and where we were going. Everyone understood who to go to when it was tough to deliver on our performance, technology, or cultural expectations. This is a very important point that I want to stress: Culture breaks down when people are doing everything they can to maintain the culture that the company is trying to promote, but they still fail for reasons outside of their control.

As a stand-alone company, our culture thrived. We maintained a culture of performance and high expectations of one another. We had a fun work environment with morning yoga and team mud races. But everything changed when we sold to GoDaddy.

Things changed not because GoDaddy, a previous competitor, had a drastically different culture—in fact, they too had a culture of performance and fun—but because as a smaller division, the team struggled to feel our unique value. The yoga and mud races were still there, but the day-to-day jobs had a new dynamic. Once we were acquired and were a division of GoDaddy, people had to come to the realization that it was not all about Media Temple anymore. Worse yet, we had to explain to our customers why we sold and convince them that we were still committed to delivering the same level of service. Losing some of our identity and pride by selling to a competitor was the first hurdle. Not insurmountable, but still an obstacle to overcome.

The real challenge came when Media Temple employees didn't know who to go to for help. When previously they could solve a challenge independently or with a local team member, now it wasn't clear who had the authority to help them. This made it feel impossible to have their challenges prioritized and get the job done.

The executive leadership team realized that we needed to align our global priorities across brands and to improve communication. We improved over time, but it required constant focus at all levels of the organization. We failed whenever people felt disempowered after the acquisition. We succeeded when people felt they were now part of a larger team and together could build on the two brands, technology, and customer base.

CHAPTER 9: COLLABORATION
TAKEAWAYS AND TIPS

- Ask your team or organization how you are performing respective to this dimension: In a collaborative company, people cooperate, share, and work well together. How would you rate your organization's collaboration?

- Provide a "use it or lose it" budget for team-bonding events.

- If you have multiple office locations, find creative ways for employees at all offices to interact.

- Create a detailed organizational chart that explains roles, reporting structure, and responsibility ownership. Do the same for each project and team.

- Encourage teams to create team values and a team purpose.

- Share collaboration success stories during company meetings.

- Invest in technologies that help employees work together and provide visibility to what others are working on, regardless of their location.

CHAPTER 10:

SUPPORT

*T*HERE'S A WELL-KNOWN ADAGE: "YOU DON'T QUIT A JOB; YOU QUIT A BOSS." While I think this is an oversimplification of an employee's decision-making process, it does illustrate the significant role a manager plays in one's experience at work.

As you probably noticed, I have emphasized the role of leaders in each chapter of the book so far. That's not only because I'm writing from a leader's perspective to other leaders, but also because leadership is a pillar influencing all components of company culture. You can check every other box of the culture equation, but if employees don't feel supported by their leaders, you will not have a high-performance culture.

Research by the American Psychological Association illustrates the importance of this point.[88] Of the employees who reported feeling valued at work, 88 percent said they are engaged, and 93 percent said they are motivated to do their best. Of those who reported not feeling valued, 38 percent are engaged, and 33 percent are motivated to do their best. I believe a significant portion of these gaps of 50 and 60 percentage points, respectively, comes down to the relationship

employees have with leaders in the organization, which is what we
will explore in this chapter.

WHAT DOES A SUPPORTIVE CULTURE LOOK LIKE?

A supportive company culture is one in which employees feel valued
by their leaders as people, rather than just a number. This happens
when employees have a positive relationship with their manager, feel
confident in senior leaders, and receive the right guidance to succeed.

In the words of Brett Beveridge, serial entrepreneur and CEO of
T-ROC, a retail sales consultancy: "One of the most important pieces
of the company puzzle, to me, has always been building my company's culture around the people who work here. From structuring
dress codes to planning group events, every decision is carefully considered to reflect what our employees enjoy and appreciate. The best
marketing tool for a company is your employees, so at T-ROC, we
have created an environment that emphasizes personal and professional growth, balance, and fun.

"My business motto is to invest in people—I'm committed to giving T-ROCers the training and tools they need to succeed and be
promoted from within. Decisions don't come down from the top;
team members are encouraged to use their own sound judgment and
make decisions according to their own knowledge and understanding of how the company would react. Always be transparent with
your employees and overcommunicate with them about the strengths
and weaknesses of the company."

In the following sections, I'll describe the pillars of a supportive
company culture that invests in people and explore what you, as a
leader, can do to make sure they are strong.

MAKE LEADERS ACCESSIBLE

In 2015, Gallup released a *State of the American Manager: Analytics and Advice for Leaders* report, which studied data from more than 27 million employees across 2.5 million teams.[89] Some of my favorite findings from this study point to the importance of managers being accessible, both literally and figuratively.

For one, employees are more engaged when they have daily interactions with their managers—through email, face-to-face conversations, phone calls, or other audio and video communication tools. In Brett Hurt's story, he paid particular attention to the most effective ways to use these tools in supporting his team. Regular touch points help individuals feel both supported and acknowledged. Managers should not only make themselves available, but also check in regularly with their direct reports between scheduled one-on-ones.

On a less literal level, we know employees are more engaged when they can talk to their managers about non-work-related issues and feel comfortable approaching them with any type of question. In addition to quick check-ins, you might want to consider casual coffee chats to get to know your team as individuals. How do they spend their time? What inspires them? What's important to them? Not only will this help managers more effectively support and celebrate their teams, but also it will help the employees feel valued as people, not just employees.

One relatively easy initiative to increase the accessibility of leaders in your organization is to create opportunities for employees to build rapport with senior leaders outside of the normal workflow.

CEO David Long of MyEmployees in Castle Hayne, North Carolina, started a weekly book club for employees. He made it mandatory, and a number of employees were leery of being put on the spot or somehow exposed in front of the boss. Long pushed them to attend, and their fears soon dissipated.

Here's how he explains it:

"Approximately ten years ago, I read a book by my friend, Dr. Tony Zeiss, titled *The Twelve Essential Laws for Becoming Indispensable*. After reading and highlighting his wonderful book, I knew I had to share what I had learned with my own employees, so I ordered them each a copy. And that, my friend, is how our book club meetings began!

"I called a brief meeting with all employees; handed out the books, notebooks, and a highlighter to each of them; and said, 'I want you to each read Chapter One of this book by next Wednesday at 11:30. As you read it, please write your thoughts down in the notebook I gave you, and come prepared to talk about what you, personally, got from this chapter. I will have pizza delivered so we can enjoy lunch together as we share what we learned with each other.'

"Crickets... Dead silence . . . Nothing but blank stares coming my way . . . Get the picture?

"OK, so not everyone was jumping up and down with joy and loudly cheering. I'm definitely not going to sit here and tell you my book club idea was accepted with open arms. It wasn't. By the way, rarely, if ever, are things that make you successful easy to do or implement."

"Then the day arrived for our first meeting.

"OK, I'll admit it! During our first book club meeting, people didn't know what to expect. They'd never done anything like this before with any of their former employers, and the last time they were in a reading group was the fifth grade, and let's just say, they did not remember it fondly!

"They definitely had reservations as to exactly how much they felt they could share, but as we ate our pizza, I set the example for our group by sharing stories from my own past to help reduce their anxiety.

"That first chapter we read in Tony's book happened to be on attitude, so I shared a story of how having a negative attitude had affected my life for a few years after losing a job. I wanted them to see I have been there and done that, too. I showed them I was human, and I had made many mistakes along the way. Sometimes I shared things my siblings and I had experienced growing up as preacher's kids.

"After hearing my stories, it seemed there was always someone ready to share their story.

"Then it happened. One by one, each member of the group felt compelled to speak up and began to open up about themselves and their experiences in life. It was fascinating to see how it just started to flow out of them. We laughed and sometimes even shed tears together as each chapter reminded us of stories from our own lives.

"By the fourth week or so, every employee's reservations to share had all but evaporated. What we found was that we were coming together as a team. People who had historically ignored employees from other departments soon established new friendships. Some even started doing things together away from the office, such as going to lunch or to the gym together."

Another version of this is leadership lunches. There are many ways to go about this, but the central idea is that employees of all levels get exposure with senior leaders over lunch. Both parties benefit: Leaders get a chance to understand the motivations and priorities of those they don't usually work alongside, and employees get exposure to those setting the company strategy. As an extra bonus, a study by Humanyze (formerly Sociometric Solutions) found that employees that sat together at a group lunch were 36 percent more likely to interact with each other later that day.[90] Dining together might encourage collaboration after the fact!

SUPPORT THOSE WHO DO THE SUPPORTING

We put so much emphasis on managers supporting and developing their direct reports that we often forget to do the same for them. What a mistake! It turns out that only one in ten people fully possesses the managerial talent to engage employees, retain high performers, and sustain productivity.[91]

We need to invest in training managers to get them to a place where they feel confident engaging and developing their direct reports. Sure, that means less time on task, and this adds more outside work on top of skill training. But ignoring the knowledge gap will cost everyone time and headaches later. Consider creating systems for managers to support and learn from each other. One of my favorite ideas is to create monthly manager meet-ups that serve as a space for your managers to share challenges, ask questions, and gather ideas.

Training managers is particularly important as you roll out new initiatives. Think about it: Managers are a sounding board for questions and concerns. It's important that they understand how to manage whatever comes their way during times of change. This is why consultants emphasize manager training in successful change management initiatives.

By training managers, you're effectively reaching the rest of the population. For example, one of the first steps Con Edison leadership took to achieve their inclusion goals was to train managers in related areas. They focused the majority of the training on their mid-level managers because this population directly impacts 80 percent of their four thousand-person workforce. Those numbers speak to the effect, positive or negative, managers have on an organization. Con Edison's case study of how they implemented their diversity and inclusion initiative is a must-read feature culture story later in this chapter.

When Chris Sullens was CEO at WorkWave, he flipped the strategic focus of the company to achieve a cultural reformation. "While most business leaders, board members, and investors drive to create what I call the outputs of business success—revenue growth, profitability, shareholder value creation—it's the inputs to the business that drive those outputs.

"While these seem obvious, in my experience, they often get lost. This happens when boards and shareholders shift focus and try to manage the outputs, while assuming that management should be left to handle the details of the inputs. This creates a disconnect that results in underinvestment in the long-term initiatives and overinvestment in strategic initiatives that make the P&L look better in the short to medium term."

So at WorkWave, their commitment to focus on the inputs became an intensely bottom-up process. Sullens recounts: "Every board update, board meeting, and internal company update was focused on what investments and initiatives we were making to improve the team, improve the product, improve customer and employee satisfaction, and strengthen the processes, systems and procedures of the company."

And it all starts with whom you hire: "So while all four of the inputs are critical, culture is created, strengthened, and perpetuated by the people you bring into the organization, so hiring and onboarding are critical. There were a number of elements to our approach that we believe were keys to our success," including:

- Developing an internal program to certify every interviewer prior to them interviewing prospective team members.

- Using Caliper assessments with each prospective team member prior to making an offer.

- Staffing a dedicated onboarding and talent development role within our talent organization.

- A signed welcome card with swag at your desk or home to make you feel welcome.

- A mentor to show you the ropes and answer any questions you may have as you assimilate into the organization.

- Employing a four-to-six-week onboarding process that includes WorkWave Company training that exposed new employees to every leader in every team within the company, product training, and a client visit, among other elements."

CONFIDENCE, CLARITY, CONSISTENCY

According to CultureIQ data of more than three hundred organizations, the condition that separates companies with the highest-scoring cultures from the rest is employee confidence in senior leadership.[92]

What exactly does that mean? Let's dig into the concept of confidence a bit further. One definition that I particularly like is: *the full trust; belief in the powers, trustworthiness, or reliability of a person or thing.*[93] A similar definition is: *faith or belief that one will act in a right, proper, or effective way.*[94]

Two themes arise from these two definitions. The first is the concept of effectiveness, which in this case means that people can fully trust their leaders' ability to drive the business forward. The other theme is about consistency and integrity.

I'll start with the former. A study by Willis Towers Watson found that fewer than half of employees surveyed reported having trust and confidence in the job being done by senior leaders.[95] My jaw dropped when I read that: only 48 percent! Then, I remembered that one of the most common complaints I've heard across organizations is that employees do not understand where the organization is going, and much less how it plans to get there. It is hard to feel confident in any leader's ability to drive the business forward if you don't know what "forward" looks like.

On the flip side, I've heard frustration from leaders of those same organizations who believe they are, in fact, sharing the company's direction and strategy. This gap in perception often comes from a lack of communication throughout all levels of the organization. Conversations around vision and strategy often are happening, just within board meetings or exchanges between senior leaders. The takeaway is to enlist the support of front-line managers to reinforce your organization's strategy at any opportunity and across all levels of the organization.

Now to the latter theme of integrity: One of the best things you can do to build trustworthiness and reliability as a leader is to consistently model what you want to see within your company. Every single thing you do as a leader sends a signal, from the policies you implement to where you sit in the office. Imagine what signal is sent if you do what you say you will do and act how you ask others to act. In this scenario, employees learn what to expect and to trust what you say. There's a sense of security. Contrast that with the signal you send if you ask everyone to arrive on time to meetings, but you regularly stroll in ten minutes late. Consider the signal if you promote the company's value of acting with respect, but you can be heard yelling on the phone to vendors on a regular basis. Although these might seem like small acts, the signals are significant.

Our study group of companies offer many inspiring examples of leaders modeling what they want to see reflected throughout the organization.

At New York-based VirtualHealth, a health care technology company that prioritizes diversity and inclusion, they "walk the talk" by creating a diverse team of leaders and hiring managers. Not only is the representation of different perspectives crucial from an inclusion standpoint, but also having a diverse leadership team demonstrates consistency between stated priorities and actions taken.

"Many tech companies create initiatives and programs to promote diversity," writes Adam Sabloff, CEO of VirtualHealth. "But their leadership often doesn't reflect those goals. We've found that ensuring a diverse leadership team helps encourage a diverse candidate pool and a fair hiring process. When a company has a balanced leadership and hiring manager team, they have a much wider perspective when reviewing résumés, interviewing, and making offers. This lets us choose the best candidate for each role even during periods of rapid growth.

"A company can achieve a similar outcome in several ways. First is to broaden the talent pool by hiring from outside the industry. VirtualHealth frequently hires from outside of technology and health care. Many companies specifically look for new hires that work for a set list of companies, but that's often how the same individuals move between the same organizations and recycle the same ideas. Beyond ensuring a more diverse talent pool, this approach pushes the industry forward with new perspectives, which is particularly valuable in a stagnant industry like health care.

"Second, forming a diverse leadership team allows that team to build balanced teams under them. This ultimately translates into the hiring managers being an important mix of genders, races, and perspectives, which will trickle into every hiring decision the company will make."

Another example is the story my friend Thatcher Bell shares about SinglePlatform, a company with a culture built on respecting and celebrating each other. The founder took this so seriously that when *Business Insider* featured the company in an article, he replaced the photo of himself with a photo of the team, demonstrating the very values that got them there.

You might ask why this is important in the first place. If leaders are doing their job, why does it matter if employees have confidence in them? The undercurrent of confidence is trust, and when employees trust their leadership, they are more likely to communicate when problems arise. This helps leaders respond to challenges that impact the employee's experience at the organization and the broader business. The same Willis Towers Watson study found that trust and confidence in senior leaders is a main driver of employee retention.[96] The case is clear: If you want to engage and retain employees, you have to earn their confidence and trust. If you need inspiration, the following feature story is a great place to start.

FEATURE STORY
SUPPORT

Con Edison: Leadership Insights to Culture Transformation

By Robert Schimmenti, SVP Electric Operations

Consolidated Edison is one of the nation's leading energy delivery companies with revenues over $12 billion and assets over $48 billion. We power the lives and livelihoods of 10 million people living in New York City and Westchester County.

Today the utility industry is faced with many challenges, such as improving the safety of our employees and the public, controlling costs, meeting increased customer expectations, managing the digital transformation, and having to integrate more renewables and customer-sited solutions. At Con Edison we see challenges as opportunities, which requires a more creative and agile approach to longstanding days of doing business.

Within Con Edison, the Electric Operations organization is responsible for delivering safe and reliable energy to homes and businesses. This team essentially powers "the city that never sleeps."

Our Electric Operations leadership recognized that addressing culture change and employee engagement was key to our way forward. Historically, our labor force has been homogeneous, from both demographic and cultural perspectives. In an operations-centric environment, a command and control culture supported a reactive and responsive approach—one that yielded good results during emergencies. However, we understood that we needed a forward-looking approach to people, process, and technology for the organization to evolve and innovate. After much study and consultation, we concluded that we needed to infuse our organization with an expansion of new ideas, new innovations, and new thinking in order to succeed. We must change how our workforce thinks, collaborates, innovates, looks, and behaves. To get there, we needed to design and implement a customized, multi-tiered Inclusion and Engagement initiative.

Our plan included a series of milestones. The first was to establish how inclusion and engagement are business enablers to Con Edison's three corporate priorities: safety, operational excellence, and customer experience. The second milestone was to showcase "What's in It for Me" through the Electric Operations management team. The third milestone was to enhance relationships between mid-level managers and executives. The last milestone was to integrate the practices and principles of inclusion and engagement throughout Electric Operations.

First, we knew we had to clarify the end goal. It became clear that inclusion was the goal, but diversity fuels inclusion. Increased employee engagement was a critical by-product. Most companies view diversity in terms of race, gender, age, and education. We aimed for a broader view that recognizes a person's thought process, work experiences, personality, cultural background, leadership style, and work styles. Our inclusion goal is a workforce that benefits from its differences as well as similarities—one where everyone feels part of the team and has the opportunity to maximize their contributions. An inclusive workplace is one where all our people are fully engaged, because an engaged workforce is more creative, willing to work across organizational silos, and take ownership for the tasks at hand.

Our second step was an intensive effort to train our management teams on how to become more inclusive by forming and leading effective, multi-dimensional teams. We focused over 75 percent of the training on our mid-level managers, who directly impact 80 percent of our four thousand-person workforce. We created behavioral profiles that highlighted their conative strengths so that these managers would be more self-aware of their personal work styles. We then developed customized training modules on:

- Managing unconscious bias to advance inclusion and engagement.

- Enhancing team effectiveness by leveraging multiple identities.

- Increasing leadership acumen.

- Developing inclusive leadership.

- Unlocking ingenuity and innovation.

In order for our management team to put their learning to work, they created action plans that reflected alignment between their direct reports and senior leadership. A process was established to ensure accountability through periodic updates.

Our third step was to leverage our inclusion and engagement training to drive better business results, develop more effective teams, and increase engagement. To solidify the links between inclusion and engagement training and business results, we created our Electric Operations Capstone Process. In Capstone, we formed teams of inclusion—and engagement-trained mid-level managers to come up with solutions for current, critical business challenges. Each team was selected based on diversity in demographics, backgrounds, conative strengths, work experience, area of expertise, and personality. Some of the team members had extensive knowledge of the challenge, and some had none.

The goal of the Capstone team initiative was to drive this diverse and talented group to come up with alternative viewpoints to find more innovative, impactful, cost-effective solutions to business challenges. We also wanted to determine the impact of inclusion and engagement training on team effectiveness, dynamics, and engagement.

To date, there are nine Capstone teams, and we could not be more pleased with the results. Recommendations from our Capstone projects, which are vetted and reviewed by our leadership team, have allowed us to improve safety, reduce our cost infrastructure, enhance customer experience, and increase operational excellence. But most important, Capstone is helping us tear down departmental silos, improve enterprise-wide communications, identify new management talent, and make inclusion and engagement part of Electric Operations' DNA.

One example of our Capstone team projects was focused on process management, where the team looked at reducing delays that field crews experienced. Through an ideation process the team sought to optimize the management of our prerequisites for planning field work: activities such as ensuring access to customer and company equipment in advance to reduce delays, enhance the customer experience, and reduce costs. The team identified some simple enhancements such as creating a prerequisite matrix to standardize the process for field pre-inspections, prerequisite status, and performance dashboards for field groups and schedulers, and system enhancements to improve the user experience for schedulers. In a few months delays were reduced by 20 percent.

In the fourth step, our inclusion and engagement-trained managers are transferring their knowledge and experience to the rest of our four thousand-member organization through a series of roundtables that focus on solutions impacting their local areas. We conducted a culture survey that has provided key information to the local management to assist in developing plans to improve.

In addition, there is a targeted Values and Respect component, designed to enhance inclusion and engagement. For measurement and accountability, Inclusion and Engagement is incorporated into our business planning as one of our Key Performance Indicators. Within two years, we expect that Inclusion and Engagement will be more than a program; rather, something that defines how we behave, interact, and do business. Based on our success to date, we believe this is a very achievable goal.

As the group's senior vice president, I've committed to transforming my own leadership style far beyond the tradition of command and control, to one that's more inclusive, engaging, and encouraging. I've gained some invaluable leadership insights:

1. Business Impact: It's Yours to Initially Establish. Early wins are important to gain confidence and alignment.

2. Say What You Mean, and Mean What You Say: Keep in mind the importance of consistent role modeling and messaging.

3. Discover Your Humble Side: Many will attribute ulterior motives and initially not buy into your goals. You have to be consistent and stay above the fray.

4. Invest in Your Own Learning: Habits are hard to break. It takes lots of work not only to educate yourself, but also to practice what you preach.

5. Release Control: Let the teams drive and innovate. They are closest to the issues and can realize greater impact if they own it.

6. Convey a Vision Greater Than Can Be Imagined: Shoot for the stars, yet allow for incremental wins.

Inclusion and Engagement becomes sustainable when there is buy-in from everyone across the board, when it is relatable to the person's workplace realities, and when there is broad leadership and personal accountability. What's compelling about this transformation is that within Electric Operations, Inclusion and Engagement has become the "new normal."

TAKEAWAYS AND TIPS

- Ask your team or organization how you are performing respective to this dimension: In a company with great support, people provide each other with the resources and guidance they need to be successful and are confident in company leadership. How would you rate your organization's support?

- Create a "lunch with a leader" program in which employees from all levels of the organization have opportunities to have lunch with a senior leader.

- Train managers in key leadership skills, so that they can engage, develop, and retain their direct reports.

- Have leaders visit different offices on a regular basis.

- Create manager support groups or events that occur on a regular basis—quarterly, monthly, etc.

- Require weekly or biweekly one-on-one meetings between managers and direct reports.

- Do a role modeling audit as a leadership team: List your values and organizational expectations. Create a system to hold each other accountable for giving feedback and modeling accordingly.

CONCLUSION:

LIVE YOUR CULTURE STORY

Thank you for reading *The Culture Quotient*. Learning and growing as a leader is a very important value of mine and one of the reasons that I persisted in writing this book! As you've successfully reached the conclusion, learning is likely a key value for you as well. I hope that you found examples in these pages that speak to your own leadership journey and career aspirations.

Are you interested in sharing your work experience with others through teaching or mentoring? This investment in people has helped me grow as a leader and a person, and I encourage you to make the same investment.

I've been fortunate to have the opportunity to teach hundreds of students at NYU Stern School of Business. My primary goal over the past eight years has been to help inspire this next generation of leaders. Teaching has been an incredibly rewarding way for me to share my experience and lessons learned as well as to provide a framework for these future leaders to eventually build and lead companies. But you don't need to be a professor at NYU to teach. Find someone on your team or in your personal life that is interested in learning from your unique experience.

I also volunteer time to mentor young business leaders for the same reasons that I teach at NYU. I am inspired by the fact that so many people have mentored me, and these mentors have had a profound impact on my life. I remember years ago the first time that someone asked me to mentor him! I was so excited to have the opportunity to give back in honor of the many people who had helped me. You too can find someone to mentor. If you're not in a leadership role mentoring direct reports, volunteer your mentorship to a student, an intern, or even a less experienced peer.

Many books and articles in the business world focus on business superstars and individual performances, and naturally we are curious and drawn to examples of superb personal accomplishments. Companies, however, are composed of diverse people who work and live together as societies organized for a goal of success. Even a start-up with a handful of employees quickly becomes a "tribe" that can struggle to find its own social code—as anyone who has been through those early days in someone's parents' basement can tell you.

The Dalai Lama has said, "We human beings are social beings. We come into the world as the result of others' actions. We survive here in dependence on others. Whether we like it or not, there is hardly a moment of our lives when we do not benefit from others' activities. For this reason, it is hardly surprising that most of our happiness arises in the context of our relationships with others."

That's what I love about the field of company culture. That's why I am passionate about teaching the ten dimensions you've read about in this book. They are codes for how to work, cooperate, and compete toward a shared mission and vision. In the context of business, these dimensions are the keys to your competitive advantage. The culture stories shared throughout this book provide rich examples of mastering these ten dimensions to achieve a high-performance culture and ultimately a high-performance organization.

If you belong to a culture committee at your workplace, or plan to start one, this book will be a helpful study guide. *The Culture Quotient* also can be next up for reading for your company's book club. Should that be the case, I'd be happy to answer any questions for your club. Other ideas include having a brown-bag lunch series with your team, with a focus on the Takeaways and Tips at each chapter's end. If you or your organization are interested in having me speak about the book, I'd be thrilled. Please contact me at greg@theculturequotient.com.

It is gratifying to have the opportunity to share these pages with readers, and now I encourage you to live your culture stories.

ACKNOWLEDGMENTS

Thank you to Jamie Nichol for joining me on my book journey two years ago as my main collaborator and researcher. Your passion for this topic helped make *The Culture Quotient* a reality. To Tony Hsieh, Fred Mossler, Alfred Lin, and all of my Zappos friends for including me on your journey and inspiring my own culture path. To all of the CultureIQ employees, past, present, and future, for your commitment to organizational culture. To the amazing CultureIQ customers and investors for believing in our important mission. To my talented editors, Herb Schaffner and Kay Mitchell, and to Rohit Bhargava and the entire Ideapress publishing team. In memory of Charlie Stryker, my first mentor, and to Josh Weinreich for your continued mentorship. To my many confidants and peers in the Young Presidents' Organization sharing our pursuit of lifelong learning. To my closest friends for your brotherhood. In memory of my mother Debbie Besner, in honor of my father Joel Besner, to the Ryan family, and to Carl Geiger. And finally and most importantly, to my wife, Leslie, and our daughters, Willa and Lana, a special thank you to my three girls for bringing purpose into my life and love into my heart.

ABOUT THE AUTHOR

Greg Besner is the founder and vice chairman of *CultureIQ*, a global company that helps organizations to create high-performance cultures. He founded CultureIQ in 2013, and since then he and his firm have assisted more than one thousand organizations and millions of employees to strengthen their company cultures. Of note, he was an early investor in Zappos.com, which inspired his commitment to organizational culture.

In 2018, Besner was ranked in *USA Today* as the eighth best CEO in the United States among a pool of fifty thousand companies. He also was named the EY Entrepreneur Of The Year® in New Jersey in 2003.

In addition to his leadership role with CultureIQ, Besner has served on the faculty of New York University Stern School of Business since 2013. He is a highly rated adjunct professor, teaching hundreds of students about topics including organizational culture, leadership, and entrepreneurship.

Prior to launching CultureIQ, Besner was the founder and CEO of Computershare Executive Services, an equity compensation management company formally known as Restricted Stock Systems, Inc. ("RSS"). He founded RSS in 2000, sold it to Computershare Limited in 2007, and remained as president of Computershare Executive Services until 2009.

In 2000, Besner co-founded Leslie Hsu LLC, a consumer products company that has launched brands such as UGG® handbags and True Religion handbags. In the summer of 2020, Besner and his team introduced SUNFLOW, a premium beach brand.

Besner has had business articles published frequently in magazines, and his interviews and presentations have been featured in numerous media publications and podcasts. He is a sought-after speaker for leadership conferences around the world on topics of business, culture, and the future of work.

In 2020, Besner completed his sixth year of the Harvard Business School Presidents' Program in Leadership. He has also earned his MBA in management and finance from the Wharton School of the University of Pennsylvania and his BA in English literature and economics from Rutgers College.

Besner, his wife, and two daughters enjoy performing service trips around the world, with recent volunteer work in Zambia, Kenya and Belize. He is also the co-founder and chairman of the Willa's Wish Foundation, a nonprofit with the mission to cure Type 1 diabetes. Besner's hobbies include health and fitness activities such as endurance sports, as well as relaxation such as reading a good book.

Contact the Author:
greg@theculturequotient.com

Follow the Author:
linkedin.com/in/gregbesner

The Culture Quotient Website:
www.theculturequotient.com

Additional Culture Stories:
www.theculturequotient.com/culturestories

ENDNOTES

1. https://www2.deloitte.com/content/dam/Deloitte/na/Documents/human-capital/na_DUP_GlobalHumanCapitalTrends2015.pdf

2. Edgar H. Schein, with Peter Schein, Organizational Culture and Leadership, 5th Edition

3. http://image-src.bcg.com/Images/BCG_High_Performance_Organizations_Sept_11_tcm9-110515.pdf

4. https://digitalcommons.ilr.cornell.edu/cgi/viewcontent.cgi?article=1037andcontext=student

5. https://news.gallup.com/reports/199961/7.aspx?utm_source=SOAWandutm_campaign=StateofAmericanWorkplaceandutm_medium=2013SOAWreport

6. http://www.gallup.com/businessjournal/204248/star-employees-slipping-away.aspx

7. https://www.shrm.org/about-shrm/press-room/press-releases/pages/human-capital-benchmarking-report.aspx

8. https://www.sciencedirect.com/science/article/pii/S0278431908000790

9. http://www.incentivecentral.org/pdf/employee_engagement_study.pdf

10. https://www.stcloudstate.edu/humanresources/_files/documents/supv-brown-bag/employee-engagement.pdf

11. Corporate Culture and Performance by Dr. John Kotter and James Heskett

12. https://s3.amazonaws.com/media.greatplacetowork.com/images/Graph_2xReturns.svg

13. https://cultureiq.com/blog/building-high-performance-culture-report-key-lessons-top-cultures-2017/

14. https://www.ikea.com/

15. https://slack.com/about/

16. https://www.squarespace.com/

17. https://www.warbyparker.com/history
18. https://ikea.jobs.cz/en/vision-culture-and-values/
19. https://www.zappos.com/core-values
20. https://cultureiq.com/blog/
building-high-performance-culture-report-key-lessons-top-cultures-2017/
21. https://cultureiq.com/blog/
building-high-performance-culture-report-key-lessons-top-cultures-2017/
22. https://www.shrm.org/hr-today/trends-and-forecasting/research-and-surveys/
Documents/Employee-Recognition-2016.pdf
23. https://www.pwc.com/us/en/about-us/corporate-responsibility/assets/pwc-
putting-purpose-to-work-purpose-survey-report.pdf
24. https://hbr.org/2015/10/how-an-accounting-firm-convinced-its-employees-
they-could-change-the-world
25. https://cultureiq.com/
building-high-performance-culture-report-key-lessons-top-cultures-2017/
26. https://www.towerswatson.com/en-US/Insights/IC-Types/Survey-Research-
Results/2013/12/2013-2014-change-and-communication-roi-study
27. Van Dyne, L. and Pierce, J. L. (2004), Psychological ownership and feelings of
possession: three field studies predicting employee attitudes and organizational
citizenship behavior. J. Organiz. Behav., 25: 439-459. doi: 10.1002/job.249
28. https://hbr.org/2015/12/
how-to-make-employees-feel-like-they-own-their-work
29. https://hbr.org/2015/12/
how-to-make-employees-feel-like-they-own-their-work
30. https://medicalxpress.com/news/2015-08-sudden-insights-brain.html
31. https://www.opm.gov/policy-data-oversight/performance-management/
reference-materials/more-topics/accountability-can-have-positive-results/
32. https://www.danpink.com/drive./
33. https://www.mckinsey.com/business-functions/organization/our-insights/
the-five-trademarks-of-agile-organizations
34. https://hbr.org/2019/05/your-workforce-is-more-adaptable-than-you-think
35. https://www.shrm.org/resourcesandtools/hr-topics/organizational-and-
employee-development/pages/viewpoint-how-to-develop-an-agile-workforce.
aspx
36. https://www.ted.com/talks/
carol_dweck_the_power_of_believing_that_you_can_improve?language=en

37. https://hbr.org/2014/11/how-companies-can-profit-from-a-growth-mindset
38. https://en.oxforddictionaries.com/definition/kaizen
39. https://hbr.org/2019/05/your-workforce-is-more-adaptable-than-you-think
40. https://www.amazon.com/
    Happiness-Work-Maximizing-Psychological-Capital/dp/0470749466
41. https://cultureiq.com/blog/
    building-high-performance-culture-report-key-lessons-top-cultures-2017/
42. https://www.quietrev.com/quiet-the-book/
43. https://www.bloomberg.com/news/articles/2014-07-10/
    steelcase-susan-cain-design-introverts-office-spaces#p1
44. https://www.steelcase.com/research/articles/privacy-crisis/
45. http://news.cornell.edu/stories/2004/10/
    warm-offices-linked-fewer-typing-errors-higher-productivity
46. https://indoor.lbl.gov/sites/all/files/lbnl-60946.pdf
47. http://www.uq.edu.au/news/article/2014/09/leafy-green-better-lean
48. Rikard Küller, Seifeddin Ballal, Thorbjörn Laike, Byron Mikellides and Graciela
    Tonello (2006) The impact of light and colour on psychological mood: a cross-
    cultural study of indoor work environments, Ergonomics, 49:14, 1496-1507,
    DOI: 10.1080/00140130600858142
49. https://hbr.org/2014/10/rules-for-designing-an-engaging-workplace
50. https://cultureiq.comblog/8-ways-that-organizations-can-support-remote-work/
51. https://news.gallup.com/reports/199961/7.aspx
52. https://hbr.org/2019/01/the-hard-truth-about-innovative-cultures
53. https://hbr.org/2019/01/the-hard-truth-about-innovative-cultures
54. https://cultureiq.com/blog/
    building-high-performance-culture-report-key-lessons-top-cultures-2017/
55. http://www.globalwellnesssummit.com/images/stories/gwi/GWI_2016_
    Future_of_Wellness_at_Work.pdf
56. https://www.compsych.com/press-room/
    press-article?nodeId=37b20f13-6b88-400e-9852-0f1028bd1ec1
57. http://healthland.time.com/2012/01/09/
    study-stress-shrinks-the-brain-and-lowers-our-ability-to-cope-with-adversity/
58. https://www.stress.org/workplace-stress
59. https://www.stress.org/workplace-stress
60. https://www.ted.com/talks/
    kelly_mcgonigal_how_to_make_stress_your_friend?language=en

61. https://www.sciencedirect.com/science/article/pii/S0165032711000322

62. https://www.springer.com/us/book/9780230300583?wt_mc=PPC. Google%20AdWords.3.EPR436.GoogleShopping_Product_ USandgclid=EAIaIQobChMIxdT9jIqq1gIVRB6GCh3YRwiQEA QYASABEgKmkPD_BwE

63. http://uli.org/wp-content/uploads/ULI-Documents/The-Human-Era-at-Work. pdf

64. https://www.shrm.org/resourcesandtools/hr-topics/employee-relations/pages/ amazon-parttime-week.aspx

65. https://news.gallup.com/businessjournal/174197/managers-focus- performance-engagement.aspx

66. https://news.gallup.com/businessjournal/174197/managers-focus- performance-engagement.aspx

67. https://www.sciencedirect.com/science/article/pii/S0167268108000127? via%3Dihub

68. https://www.ted.com/talks/dan_ariely_what_makes_us_feel_good_about_ our_work/transcript?language=en

69. https://www.bcg.com/publications/2014/people-organization-human- resources-decoding-global-talent.aspx

70. https://psycnet.apa.org/record/1943-03751-001

71. https://www.forbes.com/sites/joshbersin/2012/06/13/new-research-unlocks- the-secret-of-employee-recognition/#3dab756f5276

72. https://cultureiq.com/blog/building-high-performance-culture-report-key- lessons-top-cultures-2017/

73. https://www.awhillans.com/uploads/1/2/3/5/123580974/winning_the_war_ for_talent.pdf

74. https://hbswk.hbs.edu/item/forget-cash-here-are-better-ways-to- motivate-employees

75. https://news.gallup.com/reports/189830/e.aspx?g_source=link_wwwv9andg_ campaign=item_236438andg_medium=copy

76. https://news.gallup.com/reports/189830/e.aspx?g_source=link_wwwv9andg_ campaign=item_236438andg_medium=copy

77. The Corporate Executive Board Company, Driving Breakthrough Performance in the New Work Environment, 2012

78. https://hbr.org/2007/11/eight-ways-to-build-collaborative-teams

79. https://www.apa.org/science/about/psa/2004/06/hackman

80. https://rework.withgoogle.com/guides/understanding-team-effectiveness/steps/introduction/

81. https://rework.withgoogle.com/blog/five-keys-to-a-successful-google-team/

82. https://journals.sagepub.com/doi/abs/10.2307/2666999

83. https://www.apa.org/science/about/psa/2004/06/hackman

84. https://hbr.org/2018/09/stop-wasting-money-on-team-building

85. https://hbr.org/2007/11/eight-ways-to-build-collaborative-teams

86. https://hbr.org/2007/11/eight-ways-to-build-collaborative-teams

87. https://www.entrepreneur.com/article/278262

88. https://www.apa.org/news/press/releases/2012/03/well-being

89. https://www.gallup.com/services/182138/state-american-manager.aspx?g_source=link_wwwv9andg_campaign=item_236570andg_medium=copy

90. https://www.entrepreneur.com/article/230236

91. https://www.gallup.com/services/182138/state-american-manager.aspx?g_source=link_wwwv9andg_campaign=item_236570andg_medium=copy

92. https://www.entrepreneur.com/article/252776

93. https://www.dictionary.com/browse/confidence

94. https://www.merriam-webster.com/dictionary/confidence

95. https://www.shrm.org/resourcesandtools/hr-topics/benefits/pages/what-keeps-employees-onboard.aspx

96. https://www.shrm.org/resourcesandtools/hr-topics/benefits/pages/what-keeps-employees-onboard.aspx

INDEX